Jane Powers

THE LIVING GARDEN

A PLACE THAT WORKS WITH NATURE

Jane Powers

THE LIVING GARDEN

A PLACE THAT WORKS WITH NATURE

F

FRANCES LINCOLN LIMITED
PUBLISHERS

For Jonathan Hession

Frances Lincoln Limited, 4 Torriano Mews,
Torriano Avenue, London NW5 2RZ
www.franceslincoln.com

The Living Garden

First Frances Lincoln edition 2011

A catalogue record for this book is available
from the British Library.

ISBN 978-0-7112-3026-2

Printed and bound in China

1 2 3 4 5 6 7 8 9

TITLE PAGE A community of convivial plants
at the Bay Garden, Co. Wexford.
RIGHT The painterly meadow at Mount Usher,
Co. Wicklow.

CONTENTS

INTRODUCTION: THE BIG IDEA

'The goal of life is living in agreement with nature.'
Zeno of Elea

I spent my teens and twenties looking for the meaning of life. And then, in my thirties, I found the answer. It was in the compost heap.

The business of composting has always thrilled me. I love how the debris from a stint of gardening – the dried stems, the weeds and the grass cuttings – eventually rots down into soft, sharply fragrant, brown material. Each time I return this nutritious compost to the soil, where it will feed my plants, it is like taking part in a small, earthy miracle. The magic continues a season later, when a new generation of green things, its work done, ends up in the compost enclosure, to become yet more life-sustaining humus.

But it is not a miracle, of course, or magic: nature doesn't deal in miracles. Nature has a well-ordered system, cyclical and reliable – a fact that can be comforting in an otherwise unreliable world. My compost bays, I discovered, provide a compact example of this system's perfection. The bits of vegetation that I throw into the wooden containers are only part of the operation. Moving through them, I learned, is an entire world made up of billions of organisms, from worms and woodlice to invisible fungi and bacteria: hatching, reproducing, feeding and getting fed on, dying and decaying. And generating more hatching, more reproducing and so on: an endless bustle of tiny lives going about their mortal business.

I saw how the activity in this microcosm is sustained by me, the gardener, with my applications of plant matter. If I were to stop, this miniature world would slow down, and grind to a more sedate rotation, with far fewer living things on the wheel. The gazillion micro-beasts in their mini-cosmos would not be the only creatures affected, for so too would those who visit the compost heap to find food or shelter. There would be one less attraction for the inquisitive robins, the unexpected frogs, the plump slugs and the mercurial hedgehog (who summarily decamped next door through a hole in the wall, after too much canine attention).

I began to see that the way I manage not just the compost corner but also my garden has a direct effect on the lives of the insects, the birds, the bees and the other beings in the small

In the pesticide-free Glebe Gardens in Co. Cork, nature creates a detailed and many-layered scene.

A baby sparrow takes a lesson from an older male and learns to balance on our pond edge to get a drink of water.

patch that I 'own'. If I avoid trimming certain dense shrubs and climbers during nesting time, and leave suitable building materials around, the birds have an easier time constructing their nests. If I provide a graduated edge to our tiny pond, it makes it possible for baby frogs to get out, and for birds to stand and bathe. If I grow nectar-rich plants, I attract bees, butterflies and hoverflies (and the last help keep the aphid population under control).

It became clear to me that there is far more to the garden than the plants I tend in it, and the spaces around them. The garden has a life of its own, in which the existences of all its flora and fauna are intricately interwoven. It also became evident that the more things that are living (and dying) in it, the healthier it is. Pests are less of a problem when there are more creatures around: there is usually someone a rung higher on the food ladder who will keep the sap suckers and leaf munchers at acceptable levels. Balance is more easily achieved by this natural order of things than by my going to war with individual undesirables.

I found the thought of all these separate but interdependent cycles and rhythms reassuring – and excitingly magnificent. Everything in the garden suddenly made perfect sense, as well ordered as a fugue by Bach. Most exhilarating of all was that I too played a major part in this intricate opus. It was scary as well as exciting, because I realized that I needed to learn to play in key and with care, rather than hitting jarring bum notes. Of course, all this is obvious now, but twenty years ago it wasn't a mainstream idea, as it is today.

Nature, I finally understood, was not just something that happened alongside me. It included me.

And still does, of course. My life, and all our lives, intersect with the lives of countless other creatures and plants on this planet in ways that are both conspicuous and not. What we do in our gardens is almost immediately apparent, but our reach is also long and potentially devastating. We may strip bogs if we heedlessly use peat-based compost, or contribute to the death of the rainforests of Africa and Indonesia if we buy garden furniture with no provenance, or send clouds of unnecessary carbon into the atmosphere if we continually choose imported goods. Sure enough, nature eventually responds with resource scarcity, habitat erosion and global warming – all of which have a profound effect on our lives, and those of every other organism on this earth.

Echinacea attracts bumblebees and hoverflies, which help to pollinate the flowers while probing for nectar.

Knowing that I am part of this greater system answers those pesky questions that niggled at the edges of my consciousness since adolescence. And as a philosophy under construction concerning the meaning of life, this has served me nicely for the past couple of decades. Gardening helps me know my place in the world. Nature, I keep reminding myself, is stronger and more organized than any of us on our own. Working with it is a better plan than fighting it.

GARDENS FOR THE PLANET

'The man who has planted a garden feels that he has done something for the good of the world.'
Charles Dudley Warner, *My Summer in a Garden*

CHANGING WORLDS

As I write this, it is an exciting time in gardening. Attitudes are changing. More people are keen to tend their bits of land in a way that is in tune with nature. Every new gardener I meet wants to avoid using pesticides and artificial fertilizers. Every schoolchild knows that ground beetles and earthworms are our allies. How things have changed: in my day, little boys cut up worms to see how long they would wriggle, or if they would sprout a new head (which they don't); now they farm them.

My worm-hunting pals, however, were just employing the traditional hostile methods that had long served our species in its dealings with the rest of nature. Including gardeners: for centuries one of gardening's main themes was exerting control over a savage and unruly natural world.

The baroque gardens of seventeenth-century France were a perfect example. At Versailles, Louis XIV had André Le Nôtre turn marsh and woodland into an orderly and geometric landscape. The Sun King, according to the Duc de Saint-Simon in his memoirs, 'liked to subjugate nature by art and treasure'. And so he did: with arrow-straight *allées*, grid-planted *bosquets* of trees and clipped shrubs dotted about like embroidery on a hem. And water, water everywhere – captured in canals and forced into fountains.

Three centuries ago, however, our ancestors saw most of our planet as a great whirling pot of chaos, seething with strange creatures and plants, and rife with pestilence, turbulent elements and other ferocious energies. And who could blame them: the population was only a tenth of what it is now, and man's reach was negligible, without fossil-fuelled travel or modern science. Beyond areas of population, the Earth was an unknown, untouched place.

Today, though, there is hardly a corner of this planet where our species has not left its calling card. Our impact has been far from benign. Besides climate change, we've contributed to a gloomy catalogue that includes desertification, habitat loss, resource depletion, water shortages, flooding, erosion and rising sea levels. According to fossil records, species are dying out at between 100 and 1,000 times the rate at which they would normally become extinct. That's the bad news. As for the good, read on.

Swathes of unfussy perennials and grasses at the Bay Garden, Co. Wexford.

Trees such as this oak absorb water during damp weather and breathe it out again on drier days.

SAVING THE PLANET: ONE GARDEN AT A TIME

Can gardeners really help to halt, or at least slow down, the pace at which our planet is tumbling downhill? Well, yes, I think we can – in many ways. Although gardens are tiny scraps of fabric in the huge patchwork that is our world, in some areas they can combine to make something large and important – as in cities. Land-use statistics for London, for instance, show that 24 per cent of the space is occupied by domestic gardens; in Dublin, gardens cover a similar percentage of the city area. So in urban districts the way that gardens are tended really can make a difference. Where they are managed not just for people but for other animals and the well-being of the environment, gardens can knit together to throw a living, breathing mantle over the surface of the planet. This isn't just a pretty metaphor: vegetation and soil play a crucial part in regulating temperature and moisture, and in cleaning the atmosphere. It is for this reason that urban parks and gardens are sometimes known as the 'green lungs' of the city.

Green spaces and trees take in water during damp weather, absorbing it into their cells, like giant sponges. Then, as the weather warms or becomes drier, they gradually release the moisture back into the atmosphere, through evaporation and transpiration. This latter process is performed by stomata, hydraulic valves on the underside of leaves. When they open, water is released and carbon dioxide is taken in. The word stomata, incidentally, is Greek for 'mouths'; I like to think of the trees and plants around me exhaling quietly and benignly through billions of sets of green lips.

The combination of evaporation and transpiration is known by the neat word evapotranspiration. And the more we have of it on this planet, the better, especially in built-up areas, where buildings and paving soak up warmth – like massive storage heaters – and throw it back. This 'urban heat island effect' can lead to average temperatures in cities being 2 to 6 degrees Centigrade higher than in the surrounding countryside. At the University of Manchester, a research team calculated that a 10 per cent increase in green space in built-up areas of Greater Manchester would lead to reductions of surface temperature of up to 4 degrees. The same study also calculated that reducing green space by 10 per cent could dangerously increase temperatures. Trees, gardens and parks offer such a simple and attractive way to cool our warming planet that it's hard to see why we don't have more of them.

In the most densely developed parts of cities, about 70 per cent of the Earth's surface is sealed away under buildings, roads or other hard landscaping. In areas such as this, rainwater has nowhere to go, except into sewers and waterways. As torrential rains become more frequent, and as marginal land is developed, flooding in urban areas is more common. In these situations, gardens can act as valuable reservoirs for rainwater, capturing and recycling it.

Gardens and trees (especially street trees) also help to clean the air. Their foliage catches particulate matter – the minuscule solids that are the visible parts of air pollution. The fine particles adhere to the leaves and are washed away when it rains.

GARDENING FOR WILDLIFE

Besides acting as natural air conditioners and moisture regulators, gardens are becoming ever more important to the survival of creatures other than humans. The amount of land that is fit for wildlife is shrinking, through industrialization, development and habitat degradation. Modern agriculture has caused significant changes in the farmed landscape (which in Ireland accounts for 62 per cent of the land mass). Increased use of machinery and chemicals and loss of hedgerows have made previously congenial terrain hostile to wild fauna and flora. In a report prepared for the Environmental Protection Agency by a team at University College Dublin it was estimated that the diversity of species in European farmland declined by 23 per cent between 1970 and 2000.

This being the situation with agricultural land, it is even more critical that we manage our gardens carefully, and help fill the biodiversity gap. The individual spaces outside our houses may not be large, but – depending on what the surroundings are like – they can act as island sanctuaries or green passages for wildlife. We are the most

In our tiny pond, a frog nudges through the duckweed, which we leave to provide cover for small creatures.

A mixed habitat with trees, shrubs, herbaceous plants and grass, in our back garden.

powerful species on this planet, and the way that we curate our patches of ground can make them either a haven or a desert for our fellow earthlings.

If we plant congenial species and provide as many hospitable habitats as possible, insects, birds and other creatures will visit our gardens and set up home. For example, the following greatly increase the chances of wild visitors: ponds, log piles, compost heaps, margins of long grass, bird boxes and crevices in walls. Letting plants set seed, allowing leaves to lie on the ground and being less fanatical about tidiness make the garden a lot more attractive to many creatures. Giving up, or seriously cutting down on, pesticides may be difficult for some gardeners, but it is all-important. In a while, the mini ecosystem outside your door will adjust so that you will hardly miss these poisons. If your garden has plenty of variety in plants and habitats, it will be more self-balancing, as animals higher up on the food chain keep the lower ones in check. I will discuss all this in greater detail later, but for the moment, let me assure you that when you make your garden a friendly place for wildlife all kinds of excitement and pleasure lie ahead. My own urban plot is much richer, more balanced and more interesting thanks to the goings-on of the birds, bees, butterflies, beetles, frogs and thousands of other things that share this space.

GARDENING FOR PEOPLE

When we garden with nature and the environment in mind, it becomes apparent that it is neither painful nor a sacrifice to manage our patches like this. We soon see how the spaces outside our houses can thrum with wildlife and make a positive impact on the planet, while still being beautiful to our senses and useful for our species. Many of the elements that serve the needs of wildlife are also pleasing to us: sunny borders of nectar-filled flowers; shrubs and trees laden with berries; contemplation-inducing pools of water. A garden that is diverse and lively such as this can be restorative, engrossing, charming, calming and enlightening at different times. In other words, it can be a very good place to be: beneficial for both soul and body.

Another major function of the garden is, of course, as a place to grow food. Raising our own produce is important in so many ways. It puts us in touch with our land on an elemental level: out of the soil grow crops, which we eat. This is an exchange of our labour for the Earth's bounty that we don't experience when we're plucking food off a supermarket shelf.

Local dinner: beans, greens and eggs; and a long-tongued garden bumblebee (*Bombus hortorum*) forages in a foxglove.

When we grow crops in our back gardens, we're also cutting out the carbon load that attends commercially cultivated fruits and vegetables, some of which are grown thousands of miles away and transported to our country by air. Our home-grown produce, on the other hand, travels metres – not miles – to reach our plates. This makes it fresher than anything else we will ever taste, and because we have grown it ourselves, we know exactly what has gone into it.

As our world changes in the coming years, with a relentlessly expanding population and the further loss of arable land, it may become more of a necessity – rather than a pastime – to grow our food again. Our kitchen gardens can give us resilience in hard times, in the same way that 'Dig for Victory' gardens did in Britain and America during the last two world wars.

IN THE WEB

When we start to look after our gardens in a more careful and holistic manner, it becomes clear that we are part of a bigger system. We can see, right there, the results of our actions: wildlife is everywhere, soil and plants are both healthier and there is a feeling of abundance and interconnectedness. For example, on an early summer evening I can sit in our garden and watch parent birds feeding their babies with caterpillars found in the long grass, while long-tongued bumblebees work the foxgloves before buzzing off home to their moss-lined nests and underground burrows. A frog might poke its head out of the pond, and the first of the evening moths may appear, drawn to the pale flowers of the night-scented stock. I feel proud and happy that I've helped to create this space. But I also realize – and I know that other gardeners feel the same – that the web of life, and my connection to it, extends much further than the garden. The fact that I am a human being makes me responsible not just for what goes on inside the granite walls of my plot but for a great deal of what is outside too.

CIRCLES AND CYCLES

'Earth knows no desolation. She smells regeneration in the moist breath of decay.'
George Meredith, *Ode to the Spirit of Earth in Autumn*

I find it hard to describe succinctly the way I garden. It's 'organic', in that I don't use artificial pesticides or fertilizers, and it's 'wildlife friendly', because I do a lot to make birds, bees and other creatures feel at home. It's somewhat 'sustainable' and 'green' too, because I reuse whatever I can, buy as locally as possible and generally try to be a good citizen of this planet. But all of those descriptions are imprecise, overused and a bit too goody-goody to be offered up as 'This is how I do it, and so must you'. In fact, certified organic growers and champions of sustainability would find many holes in my practice. The limitations of my sixth-of-an-acre town garden, and never-adequate supplies of time and energy, mean that unblemished green sainthood will never be mine. Indeed, it will never be any of ours – at least those of us living in the developed world.

CIRCULAR THOUGHTS

Instead, I find it easier to say that a great deal of my gardening is about paying attention to circles. The most obvious one is the circle or cycle of life (after all, a cycle is just a circle in the fourth dimension – time). The neatest cycle is that which I mentioned earlier: where you grow a plant, compost it when it's tired out and return the compost to the soil to nourish the next generation of plants that you grow. And so on and so on. Round and round. Simple and perfect.

There are other cycles too: for instance, where you reuse grass clippings as a weed-suppressing and moisture-retaining mulch, or turn your fallen leaves into leafmould for growing woodland species, or give twiggy brushwood another life as supports for herbaceous plants. Water – both rainwater and cleanish water from the house – can be used again. Many indoor items can live anew outdoors in an entirely different role. Clear plastic drinks bottles make cloches for vulnerable seedlings; corks can be used as buffers on top of bamboo canes to stop the unwary eye being poked out. Some people plant up their old toilet bowls and rubber boots with jolly annuals (not me, I have to admit, but each to his own).

Woodland at Fernhill, Co. Dublin: a carpet of fallen leaves protects the soil, while slowly adding material as it decays. Lengths of trunk are used to edge the path.

Then there are the circles of place, rather than time. I'm really keen on these, and they govern a lot of what I do in the garden. The idea is that you draw an invisible circle (or rectangle, or amoeba shape – whichever is appropriate for your space) around the perimeter of your garden. The point of this imaginary boundary is to help you think of all the space inside it as a self-contained entity, and to try to make it self-sustaining. If you need something for your gardening activities, such as plant food or material to edge your paths, you see if you can supply it from within your domain. For example, garden compost, nettles or comfrey may all be used as feeds, while logs from felled trees or stones from rocky ground make admirable edgings.

A BIT OF BIODYNAMICS

This concept of the self-supporting plot is not my own but one that I have borrowed from biodynamics, an advanced method of organic farming pioneered by Rudolf Steiner in 1924, and now refined and monitored by Demeter, an international governing body.

On a biodynamic farm, little or nothing is brought in from beyond the periphery. The acreage is managed as a balanced and self-maintaining organism. Soil, plants and livestock are all seen as elements in an integrated and holistic structure, with each part being interlinked and supportive. All the fertilizers, foliar sprays and other preparations for the food-growing side of the operation are made on the farm, from compost, plants and animal manure. Food for the livestock (which provide manure for the crops) is also grown. Such a farm is full of diversity, but beautifully self-reliant and contained. The result is that it has little negative impact on the earth.

Now, I'm not suggesting that you should bring a cow into your garden, or indeed that a domestic patch has much in common with a farm. But I'd like to commend to you the idea of a circle that can be breached only with good reason. Or rather, the idea of a series of concentric

Logs from a fallen birch (which previously added to the tree layer in the scene on page 14).

circles, with the house and garden in the innermost one, and then further circles radiating outwards: neighbourhood, town, county, country, continent and further afield. It's not unlike the way that many of us wrote our addresses when we were little girls and boys, and first in awe of our position in the universe: in my case, it was Ardmore, Church Road, Greystones, County Wicklow, Ireland, Europe, Earth (and of course, 'Solar System, Galaxy, the Universe' – but we don't need those outer rings for the purposes of this example).

June Blake's Garden in Co. Wicklow, where all the hard landscaping is made from salvaged or local material.

So, not to belabour the concentric circles idea too much: the closer to home you can find the stuff that you need for your garden, the better. And if you can reuse the waste that your garden produces locally, so much the better too. By way of illustration, let me tell you about the birch tree in our garden that was recently brought down by a winter gale. It provided us with logs and kindling for the fire, it supplied my neighbour and me with twiggy material for our Christmas wreaths, and the brushwood became pea sticks for my garden and for the allotment of the friend who came with his chainsaw to slice up the trunks and limbs. I was sad to see the birch dramatically keel over on that windy November day, but its cycle of life is far from complete. Even after the logs – now drying in the shed – are burned, the ash will have a dozen uses around the house and garden. It will provide potassium for the fruit bushes, an anti-slip dressing for frosty or algae-slicked paving and a slug deterrent around my lettuces – to mention just three.

Keeping some kind of imaginary circle around your house and garden is kind to the environment. It limits the amount of material travelling around, which means less fossil fuel consumption and less traffic. But it also influences the way that the garden looks. If you choose materials for your garden structures and hard landscaping that come from your own plot, or near by, you naturally create a spot that has a strong, indigenous identity. An exceptional example of this is the garden of June Blake in Co. Wicklow, where all the walls, paths and other structures – the bones of the garden – are made from materials salvaged from the site (a Victorian farm) or found locally. The stone from tumbled granite outbuildings and from the surrounding fields has been reused in paving and low walls, while granite chippings for path surfaces come from a quarry down the road. Even the steel girders that once held up a barn have been laid flat to form the edging of a border. The garden sits so comfortably in the surrounding terrain that it looks almost as if it was hatched from the stony Wicklow ground.

CIRCLES AND THE SMALL GARDEN

Obviously, the smaller the garden, the more often you have to bring material in from outside, and the more often you have to dispose of items such as bulky green waste off the premises. Yet even in a tiny space there are some things that can be kept inside the circle and reused. Grass clippings from the lawn are a case in point (I know I mentioned them before, but nothing upsets me so much as seeing polythene sacks of grass clippings heading out of the circle and into the back of the bin lorry). Cut grass can simply be left on the lawn, from where the worms will pull it underground; or it can be sprinkled on the soil around your plants (fresh clippings contain about 2 per cent nitrogen); or it can be added to the compost bin. Grass breaks down quickly and releases lots of heat. It's excellent stuff for activating a compost pile that contains a disproportionate amount of dried plant material. (On the other hand, if there is too much grass in your compost and the mix has become slimy, add strips of cardboard, which is carbon heavy, to balance out the nitrogen.)

And as for that compost (which I'll talk about in detail later), it can be sieved and mixed in equal parts with bought-in potting medium. It feeds the plants, helps retain water and bolsters immunity from diseases. And, by using your home-made stuff, you cut by half the amount of bagged compost that you bring into the circle.

The composting department in a large garden.

WATER

Water is the most precious resource in the world, yet we let it flow down the drain without a thought. On average, Europeans use 200 litres (44 gallons) per person per day for household purposes, while North Americans use twice that amount. How different things are for people in the developing world, where the average daily usage is less than 10 litres (2.2 gallons). There water is usually collected by women or children, often from miles away, and it is frequently contaminated. When I think of how lucky we are to have clean and safe water, I don't mind spending a bit of time hefting it around for a second use.

Our house is old and part of a town terrace: its structure limits our water-recycling potential. In a newly built or refurbished house, however, you can install a system that collects 'grey' water from showers and baths into a basement or underground tank. From there it can be reused in toilets, washing machines and in the garden.

A more low-tech solution is simply to prevent clean water going down the drain whenever possible. In the kitchen, for instance, you can catch salad-washing and other nearly clean water in a basin and use it on your plants. Bath water can be siphoned into the garden through a door or window, if the layout of your house allows. This kind of water recycling takes a certain amount of dedication, but there is great satisfaction to be had in rescuing it from being poured down the sewer, and then reusing it in the garden.

A water barrel nestles discreetly in a corner to catch rainwater from the roof.

HARVESTING THE RAIN

Rainwater harvesting (a nice way of describing collecting rain) is another method of conserving the precious stuff that comes down from the skies. In Dublin or London a house with a footprint of 50 square metres can capture 22,000 litres per annum (4,840 gallons) from the roof. If you live in an urban district, collecting rainwater packs a double whammy in the fight for sustainability. By using rain to water your garden, you reduce your usage of municipal water (which carries a payload of processing, chemicals and labour), and you also decrease the amount of run-off that ends up in sewers and – eventually – in waste-water treatment plants.

If you are unable to collect rainwater from the house roof, maybe you can fit a water butt to a garden structure such as a greenhouse or shed. Even storing a wheelbarrow upright, instead of upending it in the traditional, tidy manner, will gather rain that you can use later. We keep our wheelbarrow at the far end of the garden, where it's a pain to drag the hose, so there's usually water in it to splash on a plant or to re-moisten the compost heap. A word of warning: don't try to move a rain-filled wheelbarrow, as the weight and the movement of the water make it disastrously giddy.

Recycled cans become homes for pelargoniums in a Chelsea Flower Show garden.

THINKING INSIDE THE CIRCLE

I've got into the habit of looking at items that have served their first purpose and asking, 'What second (or third or fourth) use can this have?' Wire coat hangers – to name one of my favourites – are particularly versatile. They may be bent over, hairpin-like, and plunged into the soil as anchors for string or netting; or they may serve as miniature flagpoles for plant labels (invaluable for marking groups of bulbs). Plastic food tubs are often just the right size and depth for seed trays, and require only that a few holes be poked in the bottom before use. At present, we have a collection of salad leaves growing in an old basket donated by a gardening friend, while lettuce and rocket seedlings are sprouting in a wine crate. And for the first year after we erected the greenhouse, we covered the grass and weeds underfoot with a fake, worn-out Persian rug that had outlived its welcome in the house.

There are hundreds of other indoor things that can be given a second chance outdoors and, equally, the garden offers bounty for the house besides food and fresh flowers. We regularly start the fire in our stove using old shrub prunings and the desiccated stems of perennials, and we bring in dried seed heads of alliums and agapanthus to decorate the rooms.

The dried heads of *Allium cristophii*: one of nature's better geometry projects, and too ornamental to send straight to the compost heap.

None of this recycling is new: our parents and grandparents brought each other plants in yoghurt cartons and expertly folded newspaper wraps. And there were a fair few tender geraniums and nasturtiums being grown in tin cans. In the United States, where I spent some of my childhood, most rural houses had a tractor-tyre petunia bed. I'd like to think that we could rediscover some of this old creativity, and dream up a bit of new, and put it to use in our gardens. But I'd like also to think that we won't get carried away trying to recycle every last thing possible, just because we *can*. There's a line that ardent recyclers can cross (I know, as I've done it on occasion) when the garden ceases to be a place of beauty and starts looking like a dump – although a most worthy one.

NEW LIVES FOR OLD THINGS IN THE CIRCLE
From the house to the garden
- **Plastic tubs and food containers:** make holes in bottom and use in place of pots and seed trays
- **Interesting boxes, baskets and receptacles:** if you can put drainage holes in them, you can plant them

Sweet pea arches, made from windfall branches and lengths of willow, at Ballintaggart Stud, in Co. Kildare.

- **Galvanized buckets, tubs and water tanks and porcelain baths, basins and sinks:** use as planters or mini ponds
- **Plastic drinks bottles:** cut up into cloches and sleeves to protect plants from weather, slugs and snails; leave caps on and use as lightweight fillers in the bottoms of large containers (reduces amount of compost required and weight)
- **Coat hangers:** use as flagpoles for labels, anchors for strings for climbing plants or loops for pinning netting down
- **Polystyrene forms and packing pellets:** use as drainage in the bottom of pots
- **Corks:** use as buffers on sharp ends of canes used to stake plants; slice in half longways and use to raise pots off the ground; use as mulch
- **Newspapers:** use as a mulch by putting down a layer of about ten sheets, dampen afterwards, so that they conform to the soil, and cover with grass clippings. Or roll into 15 centimetre (6 inch) tubes, fill with compost and sow sweet pea, pea and bean seedlings to allow them to grow long root systems; plant straight into the ground in the rolls, but make sure that the newspaper is below soil level – otherwise it can act as a wick, drying out the compost
- **Toilet-roll inserts:** use as above, for sowing sweet peas et al.

- **Polythene wrappers from magazines:** use as condensation-retaining hats for pots of seeds and cuttings
- **Plastic canisters from 35mm film:** a dwindling resource, but perfect for storing small amounts of dried seed in the fridge
- **Old woollen jumpers:** cut up and use to line the inside of hanging baskets
- **Pet hair:** leave on the bird table so that birds can use it for nest-building
- **Carpet:** cover compost heap to keep warm; use to suppress weeds in out-of-the-way parts of the garden
- **Cardboard:** use to suppress weeds, as above; tear up and add to compost heaps that are too wet and slimy
- **Wood ash:** sprinkle on slippery paving to kill algae and provide traction on ice; use as a potash feed on fruit bushes and trees; put around vulnerable plants to deter gastropods (it is alkaline, and may change the soil pH if you use often); use as a pest-controlling dust bath for poultry; use to deodorize a smelly compost heap
- **CDs:** hang from fruit trees to scare off birds

From the garden

- **Dead plant material, prunings and other green waste:** put on compost heap
- **Grass clippings:** add to compost heap, leave on lawn for worms to pull down, use as a nutritious mulch
- **Hazel, willow, dogwood and other pliable stems:** use to weave fences and to reinforce plant supports
- **Twiggy brushwood such as birch:** use as pea sticks to support climbing plants and perennials
- **Straight lengths of hazel, ash, bamboo, etc.:** build wigwams for beans with them and use as uprights for fencing and latticework
- **New Zealand flax (*Phormium*):** tear the leaves into long thin strips and use as plant ties (the word phormion means mat in Greek, and reflects the fact that the Maoris used the fibres to weave clothing and baskets)
- **Clay pot shards:** use as drainage in the bottom of containers

The ladder that stood still too long in the vegetable patch at Hunting Brook Gardens, Co. Wicklow, and became a climbing frame for beans.

SOIL

'. . . a real gardener is not a man who cultivates flowers; he is a man who cultivates the soil.'
Karel Čapek, *The Gardener's Year*

One of the curious and appealing facts about life in the garden is that the busiest part of it always appears the most subdued. It is easy to notice the activity that is visible from the ground up: the insects and other invertebrates scurrying along the surface and among the vegetation, and the bees, birds and other winged things flitting and buzzing about their business. But the real action is in the soil, in the seemingly quiescent, dark material that blankets the bones of our planet.

What is soil? About half of its mass is composed of tiny bits of rock that, over thousands and millions of years, have been ground down into sand, silt or clay particles. Also present are air, water and varying amounts of organic matter (from decayed bits of vegetation and other life forms). All of these are important constituents. Yet most important of all are the things that live in the soil.

AN UNDERGROUND WEB OF LIFE

Consider these quantities: between a hundred million and a billion bacteria, tens of metres of minuscule fungal strands, thousands of protozoa and dozens of nematodes. These are the numbers of organisms that live in a teaspoon of ordinary garden soil. Besides this nearly invisible busy bunch of organisms – which a gardening colleague of mine calls the 'micro-herd' – there are the many arthropods (literally, creatures with jointed legs: insects, spiders, mites, centipedes, woodlice, et al.), various other un-legged mini beasts and those most heroic of soil workers, the earthworms. Without these soil dwellers, the soil itself would be dead. There would be no activity of any kind. Most obviously, there would be no recycling. Leaves, twigs, insect and animal corpses, and other matter would pile up on the surface until, eventually, the world would be inundated by a sea of undecayed things.

All these soil-dependent creatures live in a marvellously complex and mutually supportive network. Their activities are simple: eating (and getting eaten), excreting, reproducing and moving through the soil. Their combined exertions act as a vast, infinitely slow-moving mixing

Composted rough shreddings can be used to mulch the soil around shrubs and newly planted trees.

machine, which scrunches up detritus, decomposes it, redistributes it and mingles in just the right amount of air and water. Yet this immense and diverse web of soil life does far more than waste disposal and integration. Bacteria, for example, are able to break down pollutants, disable pathogens and increase plant growth. Mycorrhizal fungi deliver soil nutrients to plant roots. Protozoa, which are single-celled animals, feed on bacteria and other organisms, and release the excess nitrogen to plants. Nematodes, 1-millimetre-long non-segmented worms, help control disease and stimulate microbial activity (a few are harmful to plants, but these are in the minority).

More visible to the naked eye are the arthropods, the invertebrate creepy-crawlies of the animal kingdom. Besides controlling some pests, these help to keep populations of other organisms in balance. For example, arthropods prey upon the 'grazers', the nematodes and protozoa (and other arthropods) that browse on bacteria and fungi. If there were no higher-ups keeping grazer numbers in check, bacteria and fungi communities would become overly depleted and unable to fulfil their purpose in the soil.

THE HARDWORKING WORM

Last of all are the earthworms, beloved of all gardeners, and revered by Charles Darwin, among others. He devoted an entire book to their terrific endeavours: *The Formation of Vegetable Mould through the Action of Worms, with Observations on their Habits*, published in 1881 and still relevant today. The book ensures that no one who reads it will ever look at an earthworm again with anything less than admiration. Among Darwin's fascinating facts and figures are calculations showing that, over six months, earthworms can incorporate organic matter into the soil at the rate of 20 pounds per square yard (10.87 kilograms per square metre). Not only do worms mix and bind organic matter into the soil: they actually make new soil by excreting it in the form of worm casts. In ten years, Darwin surmised, the actions of earthworms could add a layer of up to 1½ inches (38 millimetres) of soil.

Besides moving and manufacturing soil, earthworms aerate it and aid water drainage and infiltration. Roots take advantage of their tunnels, which act as ready-made passages, often lined with a highly nourishing fertilizer, courtesy of the worm's digestive system.

Earthworms are one of the signs of a healthy soil. If you find lots of worms, chances are that there are plenty of other organisms in there too. An unintrusive way of spotting earthworms is to go out with a flashlight on a mild night and examine the surface of the soil. Safe from birds' beaks and the dehydrating effects of the sun, they may be found at full stretch foraging for material to bring into their subterranean homes. You have to be quick, though, as the second they are detected they shoot back into their burrows.

LAYERS OF SOIL

Soil is naturally arranged into layers, the uppermost band being the topsoil, where most of the action of this bustling and complex world takes place. The topsoil may be as shallow as a few centimetres, or in favoured regions, as deep as a metre. Underneath is subsoil: fairly lifeless material of a different colour (usually lighter) and texture. The roots of some shrubs

Our friend the earthworm: nature's most efficient mixing and aerating machine.

and trees are anchored here. Beneath the subsoil lies glacial drift (rock of various shapes and sizes mingled with clay) or bedrock. In some gardens the rock humps up out of the ground in elbows and knees, offering picturesque, natural focal points (that can play havoc with lawnmowers).

DIFFERENT KINDS OF SOIL
All soils are not equal: they look different, feel different and behave in different ways. Some hold lots of water, others drain quickly; some are naturally fertile, some have scant nutrients; some warm up quickly in spring, others are as cold as the grave until summertime. It is possible to alter your soil type over time, but its basic character remains the same. It pays to learn as much as you can about your soil's properties, and then to garden accordingly: grow the plants that suit it, and be mindful of how it likes to be handled.

There are a couple of tests that can help determine what kind of soil you have. If you like fiddling with test tubes, buy a kit for testing the pH. If your garden is large, take samples from several areas, especially if there are different kinds of terrain. Remember that soil that is near compost bins, or that has been treated with fertilizer, lime, manure or other amendments, will vary from the garden norm. Numbers below 7 on the pH scale indicate acidity, while those

These raised ridges at Salthill Gardens, Co. Donegal, are a traditional way of managing the soil in an area of high rainfall.

above demonstrate that the soil is alkaline. A pH of between 6.5 and 7.5 is fine for a good range of plants, while 6.5 (slightly acid) is supposed to be the ideal. Having said that, I'd suggest that you don't get all hung up on pH, unless your soil swings to one of the extremes. Soil-test kits can be inaccurate or hard to read, so you may not be getting a true picture; also, many plants are fairly adaptable. If you like a plant, and think it might do well, try it. If it grows, great; if not, there is always room on the compost heap.

I do recommend, however, that you make a test pit to assess the soil's structure and drainage. Dig a straight-sided hole in the shape of a cube, about 60 centimetres (24 inches) in all its dimensions (wide and deep enough to bury a cat with some ceremony). Don't mix up the topsoil with the subsoil (there will be a difference of texture and colour when you hit the subsoil). When you return the excavated material to the earth, put it back in the correct order.

The action of digging the hole will tell you quite a bit about the soil – whether it is light or heavy, or stony, and whether there are many creatures living in it. Examine the sides of the hole and see how deep the topsoil is. Then cover the hole with a sheet of wood or plastic, and leave it overnight. The next day, if there has been no rain and there is water in the bottom, it means

Foxgloves are supposed to be a sign of acid soil, while primroses often indicate heavy soil (but don't believe everything these plants seem to tell you).

that your garden is in an area with a high water table, and is ideal for damp-loving plants. To grow other plants, including fruit and vegetables, you will need to install drains or build raised beds (I recommend the latter, unless you are a farmer, a builder or an engineer). If no water has accumulated in the hole, you're not out of the woods yet: you still have to test the drainage. Fill the hole with water, and leave again overnight. If the water has disappeared, all is grand. If not, see above re drains or raised beds. Organic matter also helps with drainage; I'll talk about that below.

The above pit test will tell you a lot about your soil. Sometimes the weeds that crop up will also give you clues. For instance, primrose, dock and buttercup grow in heavy soil; yarrow and lesser trefoil prefer dry soil; and foxgloves like acid soil. Or so goes the theory. My own garden has slightly alkaline, very dry soil, and we have all the above as weeds, except primroses. In urban gardens and plots that have been extensively cultivated, the weeds may tell a lie.

All soils are composed of particles of all or some of the following: clay, silt, sand, stones and organic matter. Chalky soil (which is not present in Ireland) may have all the above, as well as calcium carbonate – which means it is very alkaline. The proportions of the main constituents, and how they combine with air and water, dictate the kind of soil.

Heavy clay soil can be rolled into a ball (and stretched into sausages and curled into doughnuts).

Heavy or clay soil

This contains a large proportion of clay, which has very fine particles that bond readily together. It sticks to shoes and tools, and does not brush easily off clothes. Damp clay soil can be rolled into a smooth ball between the palms of your hand, and then into a sausage shape (and then, if it is really well endowed with clay particles, into a doughnut). The tiny spaces between the particles are more likely to hold water than air – which means that the drainage can be very poor. Don't try to work with clay soil in wet weather, as it will become compressed and even heavier. Remember, pottery is made from this material. Clay soil is slow to warm up, and then, in very dry weather, it can harden to pickaxe strength. On the plus side, it is usually full of nutrients and is drought tolerant. Treat clay soil with respect, give it the right additives, and it will reward you with luxuriant, lush plants and excellent crops of vegetables. If you add compost, manure or other organic material, this will improve the structure by breaking it up and by introducing soil creatures. You can also dig in sand or grit as a one-off operation to open up the composition, but this is not a replacement for organic matter: the latter promotes activity in the soil, while sand or grit only aid drainage. Organic matter needs to be added regularly (how often depends on what you are growing), as it decays in time. One way to do this is to layer it on top as a mulch, and then to push a garden fork about 15 centimetres (6 inches) deep into the soil and wiggle it a little, to open up some air channels. Do this all over the bed or border, moving the fork about 15 centimetres (6 inches) from its previous insertion place each time. Some of the organic matter will fall into the holes, some will be pulled in by earthworms and air will also be added to the soil.

Light or sandy soil

This has an open texture, so that water runs freely through it. It is easy to work, and warms up quickly in the spring. It is perfect for growing Mediterranean-type species, herbs and other plants that don't like to get their feet wet in winter. However, because this kind of soil is so free draining, it can quickly become parched during dry spells (it is especially important to mulch dry soil – after watering or rain). And, because nutrients tend to wash through it, fertility can be difficult to maintain. Some leafy vegetables may not grow with much conviction: cabbage can be disappointingly measly-looking, and spinach tends to bolt if not given lots of extra moisture. Light soils require regular doses of organic matter to boost fertility and to help retain water. This material – be it compost or manure – magically disappears after a year or so. This is one of the mysteries of gardening – where does all that humus actually *go*?

Loamy soil

This is what all gardeners crave, but few have. It is a beautiful mixture where the sand, silt, clay and organic matter are in perfect harmony. It retains moisture, but usually doesn't get waterlogged; it is easy to work and is full of nutrients. If by any chance you have this kind of soil, I hope you realize how lucky you are! But don't get complacent: loamy soil needs looking after, just the same as other kinds.

Urban soil

Soil in town gardens can be a sad old thing. Often it lacks nutrients, has little humus and is shunned by mini beasts. The older the garden, the more weary the soil. Constant cultivation uses up the nutrients; and roots of trees, shrubs and hedges suck up moisture, as does the mortar in some walls. Buildings, walls and fences create a 'rain shadow' effect, where the ground in the lee of the structure receives little moisture. Some gardens have been used as tips during the course of their lifetime and the soil may be fill of cinders, clinkers and other detritus. Our own house was built in 1838, and our garden regularly yields the contents of ancient ash pans, old medicine bottles and pretty little blue-and-white china shards. Twice we've dug up makeshift caskets holding the bony remains of tiny pets. Urban soil needs lashings of organic matter to bring it back to life.

The soil in our Victorian garden is dry and tired, but it compensates by offering up fragments of old china.

Building contractors' soil

If you've bought a house in a development that was built in the last twenty years, it's possible that the soil is far from perfect. Heavy machinery may have churned up the topsoil and subsoil, and compacted the ground in the process. Rubble may also have been buried – although if it's far enough underground that's not such a problem, as it can help with drainage. Topsoil may have been imported to tidy things up, but this might give you something like the whited sepulchre of Matthew's gospel: it looks good on the outside but hides a multitude of nasties within. I don't like the idea of digging unless it is really necessary, but if the soil is compacted and larded through with rubble, then dig you must to remove the debris.

MIND YOUR SOIL

A healthy soil is the foundation of a good garden. It produces more robust plants, and is more resilient to drought and other adverse events. What we do as gardeners can ensure the well-being of this all-important outer layer of our planet; or, indeed, it can send it into a decline. A stark example of how soil management can go drastically wrong was the so-called Dust Bowl of North America's Great Plains during the 1930s. Years of intensive farming and drought meant that the soil of the prairies, over-ploughed and unprotected, was swept away in vast dust storms.

Erosion on such a grand scale is unlikely to happen in our gardens, but nonetheless, light soil can be washed or blown away, especially on sloping ground.

Soil compaction, where the air is squeezed out from between the particles, is another possible problem – making the soil less able to hold water, and less conducive for roots to penetrate and for soil organisms to move freely. This may be the aftermath of heavy machinery passing, or the result of people trampling on the soil, especially when it is wet. Stay off your soil, if at all possible. If you have to walk repeatedly on your beds and borders in order to plant, weed or tidy up, lay down a board temporarily, or include strategically placed slabs into your planting plan. Narrow, raised beds, 90–120 centimetres (3–4 feet) wide, are the best option for vegetables, provided that you can work on them from the sides.

The great soil migration

In times past, all the soil in a given area was more or less uniform. The stuff underfoot in your neighbours' gardens largely resembled that in yours. If lavender grew well next door, you could be pretty sure it would do well for you too. Now, however, because soil may have been brought in from another part of the country, it may vary vastly from one garden to the next. Topsoil is regularly skimmed off land before large building projects commence, and is trucked hither and yon into new or refurbished gardens. Therefore, the soil in a new garden in Dublin, for instance, may have come from Kildare, Meath or further afield; that in a London garden may have been brought in from Essex, Hertfordshire or another county. Much of this imported soil will have come from farmland that has been continuously mechanically cultivated and plied with artificial fertilizers. Organic matter and soil creatures may be non-existent.

Panning, another problem, can occur when a mechanical cultivator (rotovator) is used to till the soil repeatedly. A compressed layer of earth is formed underground at the depth of the machine's blades, making root and moisture penetration impossible. Only the top layer of soil is usable, so it is as if you are trying to grow plants in a shallow container. Rotovators also chop up worms, which is a dreadful fate for our greatest allies.

Capping is where the rain pounds fine particles of soil together, so that an impermeable crust is formed on the surface. With capped soil, moisture is unable to seep downwards and rain just rolls away.

TO DIG OR NOT?

That is the question, or rather, the argument on so many gardeners' lips. I am an ardent no-digger. I believe that digging is necessary only in rare instances, such as when you are adding grit to clay soil; or when you have to remove perennial weeds, builders' rubble or other undesirables that might interfere with the pleasurable cultivation of healthy plants. Also, it's hard to harvest potatoes and to plant things without disturbing the soil.

Many of those who advocate regular digging, it seems to me, like to feel that they are being assertive about the act of gardening. By plunging their spade into the ground, hurling the soil around and mincing it up with the metal blade, they are putting manners on their plot. The systematic upheaval and the accompanying clang and wallop are visual and audible evidence of who is master around here. But digging the soil breaks up the fragile and near invisible network of fungal mycelia and worm passages: a vast underground matrix for delivering water, air and nutrients throughout the soil. It also exposes large quantities of soil, so that it loses moisture, and so that the creatures in the micro-herd dry out and die. Soil is brought unnecessarily to the surface in great lumps, which must be shattered to create the much sought-after 'fine tilth' for sowing. (No-diggers, incidentally, get a similarly malleable surface layer simply by mulching.) Digging carries buried weed seeds up to the light, where they germinate. It also releases carbon dioxide into the atmosphere. In my opinion, churning up the soil – except in rare cases – is a waste of time and energy.

I was a big digger myself until about ten years ago, when I decided to give the no-dig (or no-till, as it is called in the USA) idea a whirl. I have not looked back since. We don't dig here any more, except to plant things, harvest root vegetables or remove unwanted plants.

We gave up routine digging a decade ago and now take the spade out only on rare occasions.

My soil is certainly no worse than before, and I'm pretty sure it's better (although, to be fair, I have to admit that compost added regularly, whether dug in or not, will always build up the texture). One thing I am absolutely sure of, however, is that my creaky gardener's back is much improved, despite my being a decade older. I don't have records to prove the enhanced quality of my non-dug soil, but I can recommend that you visit the website of British organic gardener and writer Charles Dowding (www.charlesdowding.co.uk), where there is much interesting information. Since 2007, he has carried out trials comparing vegetables in identical dig and no-dig beds. Overall yields are roughly the same, but in many cases there is faster and more robust growth in the no-dig beds. The time saving, of course, is considerable.

In a well-managed no-dig (or rarely dug) garden, the soil is alive and active. Its structure is elastic and springy, and more robust than that of a constantly dug soil. Organic matter must be 'fed' to it in order to maintain its vigour, especially if you are taking nutrients out of it in the form of food crops. The best way to do this is to place a layer of well-rotted manure or garden compost on top, and to let the worms dig it in. Within a few weeks or months – depending on their numbers and the time of the year – they plough all the material underground, in a far more efficient and effective manner than can ever be achieved by a man and a spade (or mechanical tiller). Worm populations may be small in some soils, but they increase when you add organic matter.

THE BIG COVER-UP

Soil is vulnerable stuff, and is best shielded from the elements. Nature never leaves her soil uncovered, except in extreme climates, where there is limited growth. In woodlands, the earth is clothed in leafmould; in open areas, when soil is exposed, plants quickly germinate to provide a protective film over the surface. Gardening, however, is not a natural state of affairs, so we have to improvise to replicate this kind of protective layer. That's where mulches come in. When you put down a few centimetres of mulch, it is as if you are giving the soil a cosy blanket, which insulates it from excessive heat or cold and protects it from damage. Weeds are suppressed and moisture is conserved. If your soil dries out quickly, always make sure that the soil is damp before you lay a mulch.

If you use an organic material as a mulch, it will feed the soil as well as protecting it. Mulches may also be inert materials, which add no nutrients to the soil. These include

Corks donated by friends mulch a small bed (which ends up looking only a little like a 1970s home crafts project).

Shells collected from the beach serve as mulch on a pot of echeveria.

gravel, stone chippings, pebbles and crushed slate. They are ideal for lean-feeding sun-lovers such as Mediterranean and alpine plants. Recycled, tumbled glass is also available as a mulch. I applaud the idea of reprocessing old bottles in this manner, but the ensuing material looks out of place in all but the most clean-lined and minimal of gardens.

Landscape fabric, also known as geotextile or mulching membrane, is another inert material for suppressing weed growth. This is the black or grey fabric that is so often indecently exposed in municipal or office plantings, and – increasingly – in 'low-maintenance' domestic gardens. It is useful for keeping paths between vegetable beds free of weeds, or for laying under gravel. It prevents soil creatures from moving above ground, so it is not particularly friendly to wildlife.

I like the idea of mulching with found, or collected materials, especially if it keeps them out of landfill. I had a grand time a couple of years ago rounding up corks from friends, and contemplatively arranging them on the surface of a small asparagus bed, and using them to cover the compost in several large pots. My husband made unkind remarks about my creations reminding him of 1970s home crafts. However, I was able to tell him that wine corks were also being collected for use as a mulch in a Mediterranean habitat in the Royal Botanic Gardens at Kew. (This interesting nugget made no impression on him, but it made me feel better.)

Sea shells also can be used as good-looking mulches for containers of sun-loving plants such as succulents, and, of course, seaside species. If you collect shells from a beach, don't be over-eager about the task. In Ireland, according to the government department in charge of the shoreline, your collecting activities should make no discernible impact on the beach. It is illegal to collect shells commercially without a licence. In the UK, the land between low water and high water marks is considered public land, and you are free to collect shells. Restrictions, however, may apply on National Parks shores. Alternative sources for mussel shells (which look well with blueish-green plants) are fisheries and seafood restaurants.

MULCHES THAT FEED AS WELL AS PROTECT

Organic mulches are another matter, as their purpose is not just to offer a protective cloak but also to boost the soil's nutrients and ameliorate its texture. If you want to recycle materials from within your own garden plot, you have several choices. Livestock manure makes the most nutritious mulch, but not many of us keep animals that can provide in sufficient quantities. Garden compost is also full of goodness, but may be in limited supply. If this is the case, save it to add to the hole when you are putting in a new plant. If you have a bit more, use it as a mulch on vegetable beds and to topdress plants that are hungry, such as clematis and roses.

Grass clippings make an excellent mulch – as long as the lawn has not been treated with herbicides. Mowings can be put straight on to the soil, while still green, but keep the layer less than around 5 centimetres (2 inches). Any deeper, and it may turn into a slimy paste. Leave a couple of centimetres' space around the base of each plant so that it has room to breathe. Ornamental grasses, when you cut them back in early spring, may also be used as mulch; the more abrasive kinds are somewhat effective in repelling slugs and snails. Leafmould, if you have it, is the best cover possible for areas with shade-loving and woodland plants.

Newspaper (8–10 sheets deep) and cardboard are utilitarian but efficacious weed suppressors and moisture conservers, especially under new plantings of shrubs or bamboos. Their brazenly unlovely appearance, however, is the kind of thing that gives organic gardening a bad name. So disguise them with a layer of lawn-mowings or shredded foliage. But first wet them down, so that they cling to the ground. They will last around a year before they disintegrate, when the worms will bring them underground.

If you have to bring mulching materials in from outside, consider spent hops, spent mushroom compost, well-rotted manure, straw and cocoa shells. The latter smell delicious, and keep cats from digging up your borders and using them as latrines. A word of warning: cocoa shells contain small amounts of theobromine and caffeine, both of which are poisonous to dogs. Having said that, dogs don't seem to be interested in them. Our dogs, who sampled everything from electrical wiring to chunks of walls when they were young, never showed the least curiosity in our cocoa-shell mulch.

If you're lucky enough to live by the sea, you can collect seaweed that washes up on the beach. Seaweed is full of nutrients, and has been traditionally used to build up soil fertility in coastal gardens all over these islands. Use it fresh, and – if aesthetics are a concern – throw some soil, garden compost or grass clippings over it so that it doesn't get too smelly and unsightly when it decomposes.

Composted green waste is available from some recycling centres. The quality varies: the texture may be fine or coarse, or a mixture. The lumpier stuff is not suitable for vegetable or flower beds, but it is OK for other areas.

A layer of grass clippings protects the soil in our vegetable beds, while leaf litter under wild bracken shows how nature keeps the soil covered.

I'm not that keen on composted bark or wood chips, as they look a little municipal. Also, they may take nitrogen from the soil as they break down. But they won't do any harm under shrubs or on paths.

I get very ratty when I see large stretches of bare, sun-baked soil where food is being grown, as water is almost definitely being wasted. Edibles need more water than ornamental crops, so it makes sense to hold on to the moisture that is already in the ground.

In areas of very high rainfall, however, getting *rid* of water is a concern. I know gardeners with heavy clay or peaty soil in the wetter parts of Ireland, and they leave their soil uncovered, in order to get rid of excess moisture. They live in areas where the annual rainfall can be 200 centimetres (78 inches) or more. I've never had to face such conditions, but I wonder if mulching the soil in raised beds with something smooth such as straw when it is dry(ish) might help the rain slide off? Organic herb and salad grower Rod Alston, of Eden Herbs in County Leitrim, covers his raised beds in late autumn or winter with black plastic, after layering manure and garden compost on the soil. It's not the prettiest sight, but it shields the soil from excess rain, prevents weeds from germinating and stops nutrients from washing away. Used silage wrap, which you may be able to get from a friendly farmer, can be used to swathe vegetable beds in this manner in areas of high rainfall.

Our own rainfall is comparatively trifling, at around 75 centimetres (30 inches) per year. It is a challenge to keep moisture in the ground. Mulching and not digging are the most important part of my soil care regime. I've always believed in mulching, having helped my mother spread cut grass all over her vegetable plot in the 1970s, but the no-digging was an experiment. I urge you to try both.

PLANNING YOUR GARDEN

'However small it is on the surface, it is four thousand miles deep; and that is a very handsome property.'
Charles Dudley Warner, *My Summer In A Garden*

When I was a child, my family upped and moved every couple of years. At one point, when I was twelve, we rented a house across the road from the beach, along the east coast of Ireland. Our front windows, bleary under a film of salt, looked out on a small pier that, during storms, disappeared under tremendous, curling waves. The tiny space inside the front gate was bare and grey, and I couldn't wait to fill it with flowers. In my mind's eye I could see a pint-sized cottage garden billowing with frothy blooms, as the sea crashed on the shore just metres away. In a blaze of optimism, I planted sunflowers, nasturtiums and other cheery annuals, and then waited for the fantasy to become real.

Within weeks all the plants were dead, blasted into the next world by the salt air. Even if there had been no sea breezes to kill them, they probably wouldn't have survived, for I had planted them in tired soil, and in deep gloom: one little bed was under a north-facing wall, and the other was entirely shaded by the house. It was a small disaster, and it didn't put me off gardening, but it perfectly illustrates what happens when dreams and reality meet each other in an uncongenial setting. My pie-in-the-sky garden needed sun, fertile soil and shelter from the wind, yet what it got was the exact opposite, a sea-blown, shaded, impoverished patch.

Now, some decades later, I have learned to look at a plot of ground with a more pragmatic eye. I let climate, soil, light and other practicalities call the shots. It's less romantic than my earlier approach, but it saves time and cuts down on disappointments. There's no harm, of course, in having a dream garden in your head, but to bring it to life you may need to compromise. In the same vein, if you already have a mature garden you could take a long, cool look at it, and ask yourself if you are maintaining a monster. If you're constantly having to water it, mow it and douse it with herbicides and pesticides, or are fighting against the prevailing conditions, it might be time for a rethink.

All gardens need looking after (the no-maintenance garden is a myth), but there is a world of difference between tending a living, changing garden that is healthy and well suited to its space, and trying to maintain the status quo in a patch with maladapted planting that is prey

June Blake's Garden in Co. Wicklow: local stone is used for all the garden walls and for the house.

41

A mightily windblown tree: gardens in the vicinity need serious shelter.

to a host of pests, disorders and annoyances. In the first you are working with nature, which usually puts one in a good mood; in the second, you are fighting against it, which doesn't.

WHAT HAVE WE GOT HERE?

If you have a new garden, or feel that you'd like to make more sense of what you already have, it's a good idea to do a methodical assessment. Take a few hours to get to know your garden properly, and to work out exactly what that plot of ground outside your door offers. It may seem tedious, but it will make it so much easier to make the right decisions for your space in the future.

Make a simple plan of your garden: it doesn't have to be perfect, but the more accurate the better. A surveyor's tape (30 metres/100 feet or longer) will make the job faster and more precise. The plan will give you a bird's-eye view, allowing you to see the relationship between the different elements in it. Once you've drawn it, you will have captured this information for ever, and will be able to reuse it again and again by drawing over it on tracing paper. Alternatively, you may already have a site plan of your property: if so, you can adapt it to suit your purposes.

To draw your plan, first make a rough sketch, including in it the house, garden boundaries, garden buildings, paths, trees, planting, telephone lines, gas conduits and other services, septic tank, manhole covers and other fixtures. Mark in the doors and windows on the house, and all the entrances and gates in the garden. Measure all the distances with your tape, and mark them in on your sketch. Then sit down with a big sheet of paper and draw the whole thing out as carefully as you can.

Next (or before – it doesn't really matter), make a note of the direction of the sun, of the areas of the garden that are predominantly sunny or shady and of the direction from which the wind blows most frequently. The trees in the area will give you an idea of how strong the prevailing wind is. If they are staunchly upright, the breeze is benign. If, however, they all look blown in the same direction, wind may be a force to be reckoned with: the greater the leaning, the harsher the wind. In that case, start thinking about planting a hedge to help diffuse the energy of the breeze. Most plants prefer a more still atmosphere, as does wildlife: bees and butterflies are unable to go about their business if they are buffeted by the wind. Birds will be more likely to visit and set up home in a garden that is sheltered from the elements.

If you haven't investigated your soil (see the previous chapter), do so now. If it varies in different parts of the garden, make a note of that. Note also where there are changes in level in the ground, and whether they are natural slopes and bumps, or

A steeple is borrowed from the nearby churchyard to enhance the vista in T.J. Maher's Co. Wicklow garden.

man-made terraces and steps. Unless you are really lucky, there will be eyesores or less-than-congenial views that you want to hide: mark these down too. You can divert attention from them with clever planting, or you can partially obscure them with a bower, arch, pergola or greenhouse. Notice where the good views are, so that you can make the most of them. You may also have some valuable assets, such as a warm west- or south-facing wall where you can grow figs and semi-tender climbers; or you might have a beautiful formal gate that could benefit from having a fuss made over it. Or you might have a naturally boggy area where you can plant candelabra primulas, which will then naturalize, giving you sherbet-coloured tiers of bloom in mid-summer.

Take lots of photos, and be sure to shoot from the windows of the house as well. These will be your most frequent views of the garden, so it's important to note if there is something that needs hiding or distracting from, or whether there is a potentially splendid prospect that can be emphasized. Look beyond your own boundaries: is there a church spire, a majestic tree, a fragment of landscape that you can 'borrow' and perhaps echo in your garden?

CLIMATE AND MICROCLIMATE

Climate is the ultimate decider of what will grow well in your garden. If you've lived in the area for a while, you probably already have an idea of how damp or dry it is, and how much frost or snow you get in the colder months. You can also check out the regional climate information on the national meteorological office website (www.met.ie in Ireland, and www.metoffice.gov.uk in the UK). And don't forget that older and more experienced gardeners are reservoirs of precious knowledge. Their information is more local and pertinent to the business of growing plants.

Microclimate is as critical as the wider climate of a region. It is governed by many factors, including the distance from the sea or other body of water: coastal zones experience milder temperatures than inland regions, but can be whipped by salt-laden winds. The topography of an area also has a great effect on microclimate: a garden on one side of a hill may experience very different amounts of rain, sunlight, frost and wind from those experienced by a similar garden on the opposite side. The positioning of a plot on a hillside can also make a significant difference. Cold air tends to flow down and pool – just like water – so a plot at the bottom of a slope is more prone to frost than one further up. However, the higher garden is more likely to be at the mercy of the wind.

Most large towns and cities have a more clement microclimate than the surrounding countryside. Although buildings can funnel wind and create strange eddies, they also raise the air temperature by storing and reflecting heat. This is a boon in wintertime, but in summer it can be hard on plants – and on people and animals.

Our garden is a five-minute sprint from the Irish Sea: far enough to never get any salt spray, but near enough so that frost is infrequent. Some years we have none, and in the past dozen years the lowest temperature was −4.5°C (24°F) – and that on only one occasion. The trees near by, the high walls around our perimeter, and the adjoining houses give us a sheltered back garden, except for one corner where the wind whips around the end of the terrace and pulls shrubs and trees up by the roots. I suppose you could say that that portion of the garden is a microclimate within a microclimate – perhaps a nanoclimate?

Temperate jungles

The most famous microclimates in these islands are those on the south-western tips of England and Ireland: in Devon and Cornwall and in Cork and Kerry. There, the warm embrace of the Gulf Stream ensures that frost is rare and rainfall is high, making it a sympathetic habitat for subtropical species. Nowhere is this importation of foreigners more magical than in the woodland garden at Derreen in Co. Kerry, on the edge of Kilmakilloge Harbour, a small inlet bitten out of the side of the Kenmare estuary. Australian tree ferns were planted there a century ago, and have grown into eerie groves of green ostrich-plumed giants with velvety moss-wrapped stems. In the decades since they were introduced, they have naturalized, dropping their spores on to the moist and receptive woodland floor, and producing new generations of Irish fernlings.

WHAT DO YOU WANT FROM YOUR GARDEN?

By the time you've done all the measuring, cataloguing and assessing that I've described above, you'll have a pretty good idea of your garden's attributes and characteristics. (Or, let's be honest, even if you do only half of the suggested rigmarole, you'll still have a better picture of your garden than most people have of theirs.) And with the information in Chapter 6, you'll be able to work out what plants are suited to the conditions in your particular corner of this planet. In the interim, it's time for a last blast of thought. What do you want from your garden?

The fact that you are reading this book probably means that you want to garden in sympathy with nature, and that you are looking forward to welcoming more wildlife into your space, but what else do you have in mind? Perhaps you are looking for an extra family 'room', or a plot for growing enormous amounts of food, or a peaceful spot where, at the end of the day, you can escape from a stressful job. Whatever your wishes, there are still practicalities that need to be considered. Some or all of the following may need to be fitted into your space: a place for bins, fuel store or fuel tank, compost quarter, garden shed or built-in store, car or bike parking area, clothes line. All of these are utilitarian and not especially visually appealing, but it's better to plan their locations from the start, and perhaps to make them in some way attractive, rather than shoehorning them in later.

Then there are the things that you want, rather than need. Your list might include some of these: patio or sitting area, grass for play, sandbox and swing set for children, barbecue station, nectar patch for bees and butterflies, berrying tree(s) for the birds, vegetable bed, wildlife pond, privacy from the neighbours. If you have a greater expanse, you might also fancy a cutting garden to supply flowers for the house, a decorative potager, a herb garden, fruit trees and soft fruit bushes, a mini-meadow, a wild patch, a summerhouse, a greenhouse or polytunnel, a chicken run. Whatever it is that you have your heart set on, now is the time to acknowledge it. Chances are that your garden won't be able to accommodate your every whim, but it's best to get everything out on the table for discussion. Giant chess set? Miniature railway? Gnome village?

WHAT GOES WHERE

In some cases it is possible to combine certain items. For example, bench-type seating can be incorporated along the sides of raised beds. And if you fit the seat bottoms with hinges, they can be flipped back to allow tools and bags of compost to be stored underneath.

You don't need separate areas for useful plants: herbs can be grown in any sunny border, where they will attract bees and butterflies when they bloom. Similarly, many species that are suitable for cut flowers – such as calendula and cornflower – are also nectar producers. These can be dabbed into any bit of spare ground with good light, including into your vegetable patch. No room for a vegetable garden? Then grow your edibles in amongst your flowers. Some varieties, such as coloured-stemmed Swiss chard and the scarlet runner bean, are fine-looking things. The latter, in fact, was introduced to Europe from South America over 500 years ago as an ornamental plant rather than as one that gave food to the table. It was prized for its vermilion flowers and heart-shaped leaves which would quickly cover an arbour to afford

The 'wilderness' at the end of our garden, where sturdy plants and wildlife both roam freely.

shade in the summer. Moreover, according to Philip Miller in the 1735 edition of his *Gardeners Dictionary*, 'It will thrive very well in the City, the Smoak of the Sea-coal being less injurious to this Plant than most others, so that it is often cultivated in Balconies, &c.'

When it comes to positioning the permanent fixtures in the garden, you will find the plan that you drew invaluable. Use sheets of tracing paper on top of it to try out different layouts. You can also cut out shapes in stiff paper of items such as the garden shed, greenhouse, car, etc., and move them around on the plan.

A lot of good design is good sense, and can be summed up in a few simple ideas. You and your visitors should be able to move around freely and safely. The most often used parts of your garden should be nearest the house or accessible by paths. You don't want to see some ugly thing impinging on the view; and you should make the most of your best features. Pay attention to the direction in which the sun travels, and to where there is light and shade, and then use those spots appropriately. Remember, as well, that all gardens need to be looked after, so if you plan a fabulously high-maintenance space, be prepared either to put in the time required to keep it or to hire someone to do it for you.

If you have a larger garden, the parts around the house will generally be more formal. This is also the place for your tables and chairs: you'll be more likely to nip outside for three minutes with your cup of tea if there is somewhere near that is comfortable to sit (and those three minutes communing with nature can settle your brain for the next couple of hours). In our temperate climate, sunshine is something we seek out, rather than hide from, so, if possible, position your sitting area where the sun hits it at the time when you are likely to use it. Food crops and nectar plants also like sunshine, whereas your garden shed and bins don't mind being in shade.

Pots and planters should be located near the house, where it is easier to water them – possibly with water that you've saved from washing salads in the kitchen. Herbs should be as near to the kitchen as possible, so that you can run out and collect a sprig or two while cooking. Most herbs do well in big pots, but you may have to renew the plants every year to produce enough strong growth for frequent use. If you are a big salad-eater, and have the room, consider putting in a salad patch near by.

The compost heap or bin is one of the elements of the garden that you visit most often, so it would seem to make sense to place it near the house. However, because most compost operations sooner or later attract rodents, it is better to keep yours at a distance. Rats and mice are all around us, even though we may not see them. Make sure that there is a firm path leading to the compost depot so that you can dash out without getting your feet wet.

As the garden moves further from the house, you can let it wander off into a wilder mood. A natural, slightly dishevelled style looks pleasantly free and easy when it is not sitting immediately next to a house that is reproaching its scruffiness with its own tidy geometric lines. In our back garden, a small area that we call the 'wilderness' nestles under a couple of trees at the end of our 37-metre (120-foot) long plot. The ground is clothed with sturdy grasses such as pheasant grass (*Anemanthele lessoniana*) and *Miscanthus*, and with a selection of robust perennials that need little looking after. Our little urban outback is only about 10 metres (33 feet) each way, yet there are more bees, butterflies and birds there than anywhere else in our garden. When I'm sitting here, among the cascading grasses and feral plants, and listening to the varied buzzings and birdsongs, its easy to fool myself that I am in a country garden, instead of a couple of streets away from a busy town centre.

A FEW WORDS ABOUT LINES AND SMALL GARDENS

One of the most valuable pieces of advice that I can give to you about small gardens comes from an Irish garden designer, Philip Hollwey. It has to do with lines: curved ones and straight ones. Never mix the two. It's simple counsel, and it will help you to help maintain simplicity in a space. Of course, there are exceptions: garden sheds, greenhouses and garages are generally made up of straight lines, rather than arced ones. But you can still fit them into a curvy garden: the trick is to encompass them in rounded or elliptical shapes in the form of beds, paving, grass, gravel or other surfaces. Straight lines are easier to work with in a tiny garden, as you don't have to worry about creating graceful curves. The hardness of an unbending line can be softened with voluminous planting spilling over the edges. If you do go for curves, keep them as swooping and generous as possible so that they don't degenerate into nervous wiggles.

The young garden of Philip Hollwey in Dublin, where curves are not allowed in the hard landscaping; the pergola, which will soon be covered in climbers, distracts the eye from the house behind.

Paths are the most obvious lines: they are the first route that your eye travels along when you look at a space. So if you have a small back garden, think twice about sending a path as straight as a railway track to the end. The eye will rush along it like an express train, and get to its destination with no time to glance to right or left. Instead, consider interrupting the line of vision so that you don't immediately notice the end: break up the garden across its length with a large bed or other distraction, or design the space along the diagonal. Both of these devices force the eye to work harder, and make even a tiny garden seem more expansive.

HARD LANDSCAPING

The materials that you choose for your paths, patios, walls and other structures can make a great difference to your garden's appearance and microclimate, and they also have an impact on the rest of the world. Where they came from, how they got to you and how they were produced can have some serious effects on the planet and its people.

Concrete and stone

Let's look at concrete pavers, which are among the most common and useful of materials, especially as many now convincingly mimic natural stone. Although there may be recycled

A plea for a different kind of line: save the clothes line

Banned from some housing developments and shunned by people who seem to think that laundry is indecent, the poor clothes line has sunk to the same status as a messy drunk. This is horribly unfair. Those who use clothes lines are doing a service to the environment by keeping carbon from entering the atmosphere. Tumble dryers are avid energy guzzlers, having both a heating element and a motor. They release 1–2 kilograms (2.2–4.4 lbs) of carbon dioxide into the atmosphere with each drying cycle. The clothes line, on the other hand, contributes zero carbon and is easier on your clothes (all that lint in the dryer is the fabric wearing away). And the bracing, fresh, ozonic smell of clothes just brought in from the line is an instant mood elevator. What's more, sunlight and fresh air are potent bleaching and disinfecting agents – something our mothers and all the mothers before them have known ever since, countless centuries ago, woman first washed a length of cloth and hung it out to dry in the sun.

Yet the clothes line is often ignored by garden designers and forgotten about by those who are creating their own gardens. Usually, it is either foregone or shoved in awkwardly. When you're planning your garden, give a tiny bit of thought to this greenest of laundry devices. To my mind, the neatest way of drying clothes is to stretch a line (or two or more) across the garden when you need it, and to take it down when it is not in use. You can buy a retractable affair, with parallel lines that wind into a protective housing, or you can simply unhook the line from one side of your garden and roll it into an unobtrusive coil that hangs against a wall or pole. Rotary dryers are more conspicuous, and tend to suffer from the same injuries as umbrellas in a storm. If you opt for one, make sure there is enough room for sheets to blow freely without snagging on plants or brushing against walls.

I love clothes lines. They remind me of my fellow mortals' daily lives; they are the flags and pennants of a human community. I asked for (and received) a clothes line for a recent birthday. The sight of our laundry flying in the breeze while being magically freshened by sunlight and oxygen always makes me happy.

Circular granite stones, their original use long forgotten, and Victorian floor tiles are given second lives underfoot in two gardens.

constituents in some, the basis of most concrete products is material that must be mined: sand, crushed stone and gravel. This is bonded with Portland cement, the production of which emits a large amount of carbon dioxide (around 900 grams per kilogram of cement), both as a by-product in the chemical process and from fuel burning. The manufacture of cement accounts for about 5 per cent of the planet's carbon emissions. Other pollutants, such as dioxins and dust, are also created.

Natural paving stones may seem to be a kinder alternative, but they also may carry a heavy load, both environmental and ethical. At present, Indian sandstone is much in vogue for garden use: around 250,000 tonnes per year are imported to the UK and Ireland from Rajasthan in the northern part of India. Not only is the stone shipped halfway around the world, but its uncontrolled quarrying has a detrimental effect on its home territory. More disturbing, though, is that in some quarries the workers include small children and bonded labourers. UNICEF estimates that 20 per cent of the workers in a typical Indian sandstone quarry are children. Conditions may be extremely poor, with no health or safety equipment, and workers are at risk of accidents and diseases such as silicosis. Because most of the stone is sold through agents, rather than directly, it is difficult to trace its origins.

The Ethical Trading Initiative (ETI) is an alliance of companies, non-governmental

Field stone walls in the Aran Islands look exactly right in their setting.

organizations and trade unions that seeks to improve labour standards and protect workers' rights. Among the ETI members are a handful of paving supply companies. These have undertaken to ensure that all their stone is sourced responsibly, from legal quarries with fair conditions for the workers. If you are buying imported stone, do check that the supplier is an ETI member (see www.ethicaltrade.org), or honestly satisfy yourself that the products are ethically sourced. If the stone seems a steal, it probably is – with underage and bonded labourers in an illegal quarry paying a price with their health and quality of life.

There are alternatives to imported stone. If you buy from a quarry in your region, the product requires far less transport and its processing provides local jobs. Stone that is indigenous to the region also looks more at home in the landscape and makes your garden look as if it grew out of the area, instead of having been shipped in from far-off places. True sustainability advocates, however, would argue that stone that is attached to the earth should stay where it is, as quarrying causes pollution and leads to a loss of natural habitat. It is definitely kinder to the planet to use recycled paving slabs, cobbles and bricks; these can be found at salvage companies. If you have a larger property with old buildings that have collapsed or are dangerous, consider reusing the stone in the garden. If you are using new material, use as little as possible. Look also for concrete products that use high proportions of reclaimed matter.

Paving the way to disaster

The laying of hard surfaces in gardens – for car parking and in the quest for less maintenance – has been progressing at a gallop for the last couple of decades. Research by the Royal Horticultural Society has shown that in north-east England nearly a quarter of front gardens are completely paved in. And in 2005, a report by the London Assembly Environment Committee noted that 12 square miles of front gardens are now under paving in the British capital – that's the equivalent of twenty-two Hyde Parks. I don't have statistics for Ireland's major cities, but anyone can see that Irish gardens are also being sealed in by an ever-advancing crust of paving.

What's wrong with this? Well, aside from the barren appearance that an unrelieved stretch of paving, concrete or tarmac gives to a garden, there are other negative impacts. In urban areas, rainwater run-off can create serious problems. Normally, the soil in a garden acts as a giant sponge, and is capable of holding a large amount of moisture – which is then taken up by plants and given back to the atmosphere. Where the ground has been covered over with an impenetrable material, rain has nowhere to go, except into the municipal drains. In neighbourhoods where many householders have locked away the soil in their front gardens, the extra volume of water may be considerable. Flash flooding, a phenomenon of which we have seen plenty in recent years, may occur. There is also undue pressure on sewage plants, and this may result in pollution of watercourses and the sea. Soil that is deprived of moisture by a skin of paving starts to shrink, which can cause subsidence and cracking in paths, walls and even houses.

In Britain, recent legislation states that householders must seek planning permission for new or replacement driveways unless they are made of a water-penetrable surface such as gravel,

Heath pearlwort (*Sagina subulata*) can be used as ground cover in small areas. It needs constant weeding while it becomes established, so large expanses are time-consuming.

permeable paving or porous asphalt, or unless the rainwater is directed to a lawn or border to drain naturally. At the time of writing, similar legislation is pending in Ireland.

Expanses of paving, brick, concrete and other hard surfaces – permeable or not – also act as giant heaters, absorbing warmth during the day and throwing it back at night, making conditions unpleasant in summer. Paved-in gardens preclude the growing of plants, and with no foliage to capture dust and other pollution the air quality suffers – which can give rise to respiratory disorders. And of course, if there are no plants, there is nowhere for wildlife to feed or shelter. The paved-in garden is a disaster for man, beast and planet.

Gardening for cars

Where parking is not available on the street, space must be made for the car in the front garden. But there is no need to seal in the entire space: with a little thought, cars and plants may peacefully coexist. First, the best place for parking is not necessarily bang in front of the hall door. If the garden is sufficiently long, you can park adjacent to the road and leave room for a planted area next to the house. Put in a partial barrier such as a trellis, hedge or clump of bamboos to prevent your eye from immediately alighting on the car bumper the minute you exit the house.

If the garden is smaller, with the car taking up the lion's share of the space, you don't need to surface the whole plot. Only the tyres touch the ground, so you can lay a pair of 'tracks' made from paving blocks or slabs. The nice thing about this is that you can put low-growing plants in the gap between the tracks. As long as they are exposed to light for a few hours every day, they will be fine. Gravel is also a good surface for car parking, as it is completely water-permeable. You can plant right into it too, using Mediterranean-type species, which will enjoy the reflected heat. Just make sure that the spot that is going to bear the weight of the car is good and firm. You may need to put in a layer of hardcore for support, and then bash it down with a vibrating plate compactor.

Low-growing plants for underneath cars
- Bugle (*Ajuga reptans*)
- Black mondo grass (which is actually a lily: *Ophiopogon planiscapus* 'Nigrescens')
- Low-growing grasses such as miniature sedges (*Carex*) and fescues (*Festuca*)
- Small-leaved ivies (*Hedera helix* spp.)
- Lesser periwinkle (*Vinca minor*)
- Compact hardy geraniums, such as *G. traversii* and *G. cinereum* 'Ballerina'
- Creeping thyme (*Thymus serpyllum*) and Corsican mint (*Mentha requienii*)
- Deadnettle (*Lamium maculatum*)
- Miniature bulbs, such as crocus, small cyclamen and snowdrop
- Low-growing succulents such as the smaller *Echeveria* and *Sempervivum*

A retaining wall made from laurel trunks; and the little table which I rescued from a skip.

WOOD IN THE GARDEN

Timber is one of the most compatible materials that you can use in the garden. Having once been a plant itself, it strikes up a rapport with living plants. Wooden trellises, pergolas, fences, obelisks, furniture: all look at home amongst the greenery. Trees absorb carbon dioxide while they are growing, and if more are replanted after they are felled, they are an infinite and sustainable resource. Wood from trees that you grow and replant yourself carries little environmental and ethical baggage: it has metres – not miles – to travel, and there has been no dodgy dealing in the transfer of resources.

An equally good choice is second-hand or waste timber: from friends, salvage yards or recycling groups such as Freecycle. We keep a keen eye on skips in our neighbourhood, and on piles of wood on their way to the dump. Our three compost bins are built of planks that were once part of a set for a photographic shoot. I rescued the little table on our patio half a dozen years ago from a skip: it needed only a coat or two of paint to revive it, and has since hosted many convivial lunches and cocktail hours.

But we don't all have room to be growing trees, or the time and energy to go skip diving for raw material for our garden structures and furniture. Nor do we all have the expertise to make our own bits and pieces. So the next best thing is to buy locally grown and manufactured timber products. In some cases, you may know the maker and the source of the wood. It could be a woodworker who patronizes the local sawmill, which in turn processes wood grown in the

Forest Stewardship Council

The FSC (www.fsc.org) is an international, non-governmental, not-for-profit organization that promotes the management of forests and the harvesting of their timber in a sustainable and socially responsible manner. It was set up in the 1990s in response to the growing problem of global deforestation. Illegal and unregulated logging, especially in tropical forests, destroys both the habitat and the livelihood of forest-dwelling people. And it threatens the biodiversity of this planet, as tropical forests are spectacularly rich in species. Cutting down forests also releases massive amounts of carbon dioxide into the atmosphere: around a fifth of the world's annual carbon emissions are from deforestation.

Forest products from operations that meet a set of agreed standards are certified by the FSC and bear labels to this effect. The organization states that producers must ensure that forests are 'managed to meet the social, economic, ecological, cultural and spiritual needs of present and future generations'.

The FSC has its critics, though. Small producers say that its bureaucracy can be too weighty and costly for modest enterprises. Also, FSC-Watch (www.fsc-watch.org) maintains that the organization is not as transparent as it should be, and that some of its certifications fall well short of its purported standards. The state-run monocultural and clear-felled Sitka spruce plantations in Ireland are among the contentious certifications.

area. If you are uncertain about the provenance of timber, look for Forest Stewardship Council (FSC) certification or other accreditation (but see the box on page 55).

The further outside your immediate circle that timber products originate, the greater the impact that their transport makes on the environment. Hardwood garden furniture can be particularly problematic, as much of it comes from areas in the developing world where there is extensive illegal logging. A report by the Environmental Investigation Agency in 2008 states that there is a thriving garden furniture business in Vietnam using smuggled wood from elsewhere in Asia, with the end products being destined for European consumers. In many cases the furniture bears false certification. Other wood for outdoor tables and chairs may come from the Democratic Republic of Congo, where there is large-scale illegal logging. At present, while there is widespread crime relating to forest products, it is difficult to tell whether imported hardwood garden furniture has been responsibly manufactured.

Hardwood decking may have similarly unreliable origins, so if you are thinking of installing some do ask many questions about it first. Be aware also that decking offers a cosy, dry environment for rodents underneath it, and if it adjoins your house, it brings them a quick scurry from indoors. I'm not anti-decking – it is a smart surface for outside contemporary houses – but it is a welcome mat for unwelcome visitors.

THE GREEN, GREEN GRASS

A perfect lawn is a beautiful thing indeed: a green velveteen pause that acts as a moment of calm in the hurly-burly of life. Yet such serenity is achieved at a price. A 'proper' grass lawn is a monoculture, and cannot be maintained without chemicals. Artificial fertilizers are used to green it up, and selective herbicides are required to kill off the broad-leaved plants that try to colonize it – including lawn daisies, the raw material for children's daisy-chains. Pesticides may be called upon to kill leatherjackets (the larvae of craneflies) and chafer grubs. Earthworms, moreover, are unwelcome, on account of the worm casts that they leave on the pristine surface. Lawns need watering in dry weather to stay green, and they need constant maintenance. The petrol lawnmower is not an environmentally friendly machine.

Having said all that, grass is the perfect surface for children to play on and for people of all ages to loll on. And if you leave out pesticides, it attracts thrushes and other birds, who forage in it for larvae and worms. Forget the herbicides, and the daisies and other flowering 'weeds' return, as do the more personable invertebrates, such as bees, butterflies and beetles. If you reduce the size of a lawn, you can mow it with a push mower, which is excellent exercise and cuts out fuel consumption and carbon emissions. If you keep the edges of the grass tidy, it will retain its character as a smart green foil to the rest of the garden. Watering lawns is a waste of a precious resource, and it's not necessary for the well-being of the grass. Yes, the grass will turn beige in very dry weather, but it will recover quickly.

Another way of dealing with grass is to treat it as a meadow. Start from scratch and sow a mixture that is suitable for your soil. Or you can make do with your existing grass and augment it with wild flower plantlets and bulbs. This was the method favoured by the late great gardener and writer Christopher Lloyd. He made several meadows from existing grassland at Great

If you have the room, why not manage your grass as a meadow? It's prettier than a lawn, and much more interesting to wildlife.

Dixter in East Sussex, including one that he established on his father's putting green. Even if you have a tiny meadow, keep a path mown through it, to contrast with and enhance the free-spirited character of the long grass and flowers. Meadows must be mown two or three times a year and the clippings removed to keep the soil fertility from building up.

HEDGES: LIVING BOUNDARIES

When I was a teenager, we rented a house for a short period that was surrounded by high laurel hedges, and where the garden was further divided by more hedges. Our tenancy agreement stipulated that we would maintain them – a chore that fell largely to my father, who, as a writer, had heretofore led more a life of the mind than of the garden. There were yards and yards of hedges, as my mother reported to my sister in a letter: 'I measured the hedge on one side and it's fifty yards, which means we have approx 200 yards on the perimeter, plus extra, gratuitous hedges inside, cutting the lawn into segments, screening the compost heap, and also an infant maze in one corner . . .'

All had to be cut, and this was in the days before electric trimmers. Worst of all were the roadside hedges, up to 14 feet high (measured again by my horrified mother). She explained to my sister in another letter: 'Took out one of our wooden packing cases and put the step ladder

Staggered beech hedges give a tantalizing hint of a further garden.

on top of that. While I held the ladder, Daddy cut off three foot shoots from the top.' As my parents performed this embarrassing double act out in front (everyone else on the road had proper gardeners), my brother was elsewhere in hedge hell, doggedly clipping away.

Fully two and a half months after the packing case and ladder had made their appearances, my father complained in a letter to friends in America: 'I am heavily engaged with the hedges at Blairfinde, my hands and arms a mass of scratches.' Each hedge, he noted miserably, 'has two sides and a top, a three-way operation, you might say'.

He spread his pain freely across his correspondence, tapping out hedge letters during the day, when he should have been writing his novel. And in the evening, the petulant snip-snip-snip of the clippers and his suffering sighs were the soundtrack for most of spring and summer. We stayed for only nine months in that house, departing before the next clipping season.

Although I escaped hedge duty, it was a long time before I was able to look at a clipped row of shrubs with anything other than jaded apprehension. Now, however, ensconced at a safe distance in middle age, I have to declare myself a hedge enthusiast.

Why a hedge?

A hedge, if you have the space, is the very best boundary or dividing material for a garden. It is the ultimate low-impact, environmentally friendly structure. Unlike walls or fences, its establishment and maintenance require no carbon-heavy cement or blocks, and no pollutant-creating preservatives or paints. If you clip it by hand, it uses no energy to maintain except your own. Having said that, if there's more hedge than you can cut in an afternoon, a power trimmer might keep someone in the house from feeling martyred. Remember not to clip during the nesting season, from early spring until mid-summer, and be careful about clipping berry-bearing hedges – delay until after the fruits have been eaten. Conifers should be clipped before September (or October in mild areas), as later trimming can often lead to die-back and ugly brown patches.

Unlike a solid fence or wall, a hedge diffuses and absorbs the wind, rather than bouncing it off to somewhere else. Its leaves and branches act as a filter, for both dust and noise, which makes it a useful barrier between house and road (beech, however, is not always happy by urban roads). A hedge is cheaper than most other boundaries, and lasts decades, or even centuries. The box hedges at Birr Castle in Ireland, for instance, date from the seventeenth century, and are the tallest box hedges in the world. (In fact, they'd probably look better if they were trimmed, but there is a world record at stake there.)

A hedge offers privacy in a less aggressive way than a high wall, and if you want to deter intruders, thorny or spiny species such as holly, berberis, pyracantha and *Rosa rugosa* will do the trick. Trimming such a boundary is not a bundle of fun, though, and demands snag-proof clothing and leather gloves. In the country, well-knit hedges of hawthorn and blackthorn are used to keep animals out (or in).

But the main factor that makes the hedge superior to the wall or fence is that it is a living thing, changing throughout the year, and providing an always interesting comment on the seasons: from spring's new leaves, to the flowers and fruit that may follow and through to the last leaves and bare twigs as the year winds down. Even a stolid evergreen such as griselinia, which looks much the same in summer as in winter, is teeming with life. A hedge offers a safe place for the seasonal dramas of the garden's feathered inhabitants: from hopeful egg to secretive fledgling to mature adult. And food, of course, is readily at hand (or beak) in the resident invertebrates and – in some species – fruits.

Planting a hedge

Most hedges start out life as bundles of bare-rooted, two- or three-year-old saplings. These should be planted while they are dormant, which is, roughly, from November to April. The period will vary according to your area. Plant only when the soil is workable, and not waterlogged or hard frozen. Young plants have more vigour and are more resilient than larger, older ones. They will always establish better, and will be more dense and less gappy, especially at the base. If plants are containerized, they may be planted at any time of the year, but they will need more care, and plenty of watering in dry weather.

The planting operation is akin to making a good foundation for a building, so it's important to give it your all. Start with clean ground, free from weeds and grass. Dig a trench at least 30 centimetres (12 inches) deep and 45 centimetres (18 inches) wide for a single row of plants, or twice the width for a double row (if you are using a double row, stagger the plants so that they fill out more evenly). Don't overwork heavy soil, as the particles will bind together to make the base and sides of your trench impenetrable to drainage, like a long clay bathtub. If necessary, break up the base with a fork or mattock. Add plenty of garden compost, well-rotted farmyard manure or other organic material, to improve the soil structure and vigour. Add sharp sand or grit if the soil is poorly drained. If you are using bare-rooted plants, look for the 'tide mark' on the stems for the previous soil level, and plant at the same depth. Water well after planting, to settle the soil around the roots.

After planting, keep the base of the hedge free from other growth, including weeds and grass, as these will fight it for nutrients and moisture. A mulch of landscape fabric, cardboard or even several layers of newspaper will do the job – but do make sure to cover it with something less unsightly. Ideally, use a mulch that will feed as well as protect: well-rotted manure or grass clippings (which can be used fresh). Make sure that the ground is damp before you mulch. During the first couple of years, check in dry weather that the soil is still slightly moist under the mulch. If not, water well so that the moisture soaks into the soil.

Before the start of the second growing season, your hedge will need its formative pruning. (Some gardeners prefer to do this when planting, but the Royal Horticultural Society now recommends waiting.) Deciduous plants should be cut back to about half their height in winter, and evergreens to about two-thirds, in spring. This helps promote basal growth, so that the hedge doesn't grow up to have bare legs. Give a yearly feed: a sprinkle of pelleted chicken manure or a mulch of other nutritious material such as well-rotted manure or garden compost. An exception to this rule is beech, according to my hedge-mistress friend Frances MacDonald. She recommends letting beech grow until it is 30 centimetres (12 inches) past the height that you are aiming for, which will take some years (the sides can be trimmed after the first year). Then you cut it 15 centimetres (6 inches) above the required height, and at each subsequent cutting, you gradually lower it. This method gives the hedge a dense and well-shaped top, but it works only if you can get good, strong-growing plants.

HEDGE SPECIES FOR SPECIAL PURPOSES

Remember, you can mix species for a less formal look. If you include flowering and fruiting species, the wildlife value of the hedge will be increased.

Moist sites

But not waterlogged or poorly drained

- Alder, including Italian alder (*Alnus cordata*), common alder (*A. glutinosa*) grey alder (*A. incana*): deciduous; catkins and cone-like structures are attractive to birds; plant 60cm (24in) apart
- Hornbeam (*Carpinus betulus*): deciduous, but retains old leaves for the first part of winter; plant 45cm (18in) apart

- Hawthorn (*Crataegus monogyna*): deciduous; spiny; frothy white flowers and red fruits; good for birds and bees; plant 30cm (12in) apart
- Snowberry (*Symphoricarpos* spp.): deciduous; small pink-flushed flowers and white berries; plant 45–60cm (18–24in) apart
- Western red cedar (*Thuja plicata*): evergreen conifer; aromatic leaves; a good substitute for the un-neighbourly and ungainly leylandii, as it can be pruned back to old wood; plant 60cm (24in) apart
- Holly (*Ilex* spp.): evergreen, spiny leaves; berries are attractive to birds; plant 45–60cm (18–24in) apart

Cold, exposed sites

In very windy sites, erect a windbreak until the hedge establishes
- Hazel (*Corylus avellana*): deciduous; yellow catkins; good for wildlife; plant 60–90 cm (24–36in) apart
- Beech (*Fagus sylvatica*): deciduous, but retains dead leaves over winter; plant 45cm (18in) apart
- Blackthorn or sloe (*Prunus spinosa*): deciduous; very spiny; white flowers and black fruits; good for wildlife; plant 45cm (18in) apart
- Yew (*Taxus baccata*): dense, dark green evergreen; red fruits are attractive to birds; cannot tolerate wet soil; foliage is poisonous to animals: do not use near livestock; plant 45cm (18in) apart. Also hornbeam, hawthorn, holly and western red cedar: see above.

Western red cedar (*Thuja plicata*) is superior to leylandii for hedging: it can be pruned back to old wood and the foliage is pleasantly aromatic.

A griselinia hedge, cut into waves at a coastal garden.

Shady sites

- Barberry (*Berberis* spp.): most are evergreen (*B. thunbergii* is not) with small prickly leaves; yellow or orange flowers; blue or red fruits; plant 45–60cm (18–24in) apart
- Box (*Buxus sempervirens*): evergreen, tiny leaves; plant 23–38 cm (9–15in) apart
- Laurel, both Portugal laurel (*Prunus lusitanica*) and cherry laurel (*P. laurocerasus*): evergreen, large, glossy leaves; plant 45–60cm (18–24in) apart
- Firethorn (*Pyracantha* spp.): evergreen; spiny; white flowers and red, orange or yellow berries; berries are best in brighter positions; good for bees and birds; plant 60cm (24in) apart
- Flowering currant (*Ribes sanguineum*): deciduous; pink flowers and dark blue berries; distinctive odour (not far off cat pee); good bee and bird plant
- Also alder, holly, snowberry, yew.

Coastal sites and dry soil

- With dry soil, add plenty of organic matter when planting and keep the soil lightly moist for the first couple of years
- Griselinia (*Griselinia littoralis*): evergreen; lime-coloured, waxy leaves; plant 60cm (24in) apart
- *Escallonia* cvs: evergreen; dark green, shiny leaves; pink tubular flowers; plant 45–60cm (18–24in) apart

Rosa rugosa has crinkled foliage and shiny hips which birds will eat in late autumn.

- *Fuchsia* 'Riccartonii': for milder areas; deciduous; pink flowers; plant 45cm (18in) apart
- Rugosa rose (*Rosa rugosa*) and its cultivars, such as 'Blanc Double de Coubert' and 'Fru Dagmar Hastrup': deciduous; leathery, wrinkled leaves; pink, white or red flowers; terracotta-coloured hips, beloved of birds; plant 30–60cm (12–24in) apart
- *Olearia* spp.: for milder areas; greyish leaves; daisy-like flowers; plant 45–60cm (18–24in) apart
- Also alder, hawthorn, holly, blackthorn, snowberry

Fedges

A fedge is a cross between a fence and a hedge, made from fresh willow rods stuck into the ground in early spring. The rods root and soon become a living fence. As the years go by, new shoots can be woven in or pruned out. I've never seen a fedge older than ten years, so am not sure whether they can be long lasting, and still maintain their shape. Great fun for children, though.

PLANTS

Out of the soil the buds come,
The silent detonations
Of power wielded without sin.
R.S. Thomas, *The Garden*

You can't have a garden without plants. They are the flesh and blood on the bones of the garden. You might also say that they are the fine clothing as well, with their exquisite flowers and gleaming fruits. You could add that they are the sensible outerwear, providing shelter from strong winds and cover from rain. You *could* say all these things, but really, no metaphor is adequate to describe the importance of plants to the space outside your door.

Plants are the garden. They are a vital element in its ecology. They provide protection and lodgings for many creatures; entire colonies of insects can live on a single shrub or branch, and in turn give sustenance to other insects, and to birds. Plants supply nectar and pollen for bees, butterflies, moths and other insects; fruits and seeds for birds and mammals; leaves and bark for creatures great and small. Even when they are dead, decaying plants become food for woodlice, worms and countless other detritivores.

Plants also act as regulators of the climate, absorbing and transpiring water, cooling and cleaning the air, casting shade and offering a buffer from cold and damaging winds. They protect the soil with their foliage and stabilize it with their roots. They are pleasing to us humans: lovely to look at, to smell, to feel, to hear, and – of course – to eat. Without plants we would be dead.

THE RIGHT PLANT

There's one big rule for choosing plants, as far as I'm concerned. And that is: grow only what suits your climate and conditions. It is possible to cultivate inappropriate plants – for example, tree ferns in dry soil, or lavender in heavy, poorly drained clay – but only by adjusting the conditions: you need to lavish water on the first, and to dig a ton of grit into the second. And even so, in a year or two such unsuitable species will most likely have expired, or be waiting bad-temperedly for someone to put them out of their misery.

Late summer colour at the Dillon Garden in Dublin, with the meadowsweet *Filipendula rubra* 'Venusta' forming pink clouds that drift above the border.

An exception to the rule – that many Irish and British gardeners practice – is to take a chance on plants that are a little more delicate than your garden's climate allows. Give them your warmest and most sheltered spot. You'll get away with such impertinence in some years, and the sight of such exotics will give you a lovely satisfied glow (and some bragging rights). In less fortunate years, the winter will see your tender treasures turn to mush, from frost or from wet feet. But their passing on to the compost heap opens up that desirable thing, especially in a small garden: a planting opportunity. In our garden the mourning period for lost plants is usually short: within hours I'm trying to work out what better and more interesting plant I can try in the recently deceased's place.

So allow yourself the odd gamble with species of borderline hardiness (because we all enjoy a bit of a challenge), but otherwise, plant for your climate and conditions. Your garden will be more comfortable in its skin, and the plants, being from roughly similar habitats, will look well together and form a sympathetic community. The garden will also be healthier, with the plants being better able to withstand whatever extremes the weather throws at them. If you have dry soil, and you plant Mediterranean-type species, they will handle drought with more grace than big-leaved water hogs. If you have damp soil, and you plant moisture-lovers, they won't drown if your garden is temporarily flooded. Our changing climate ensures that we will be getting a lot more drastic weather events in the coming years – so we would do well to make our gardens more resilient during such occurrences by planting in this way.

SEASONS

Besides choosing appropriate plants for your soil and climate, think about making the garden interesting at different seasons – both for you and for the creatures that you share your plot with. It is easy to have flowers and berries during the middle half of the year. Visits to the garden centre are more frequent then, and plants that put on a show during that period tend to hop into our trolleys and baskets. But that can leave the garden too quiet in the chilly months. All it takes to shake the winter garden awake is a shrub or tree in blossom: a daphne, say, or a winter-flowering cherry. It will bring cheer to the weary human spirit during the cold season, and be a life saver for the bumblebee, which – unlike the honeybee – does not build up a significant food store in its nest. (For suggestions of plants for particular seasons, see Chapter 11.)

PLACES

Where you put a plant is just as crucial as what that plant is. Obviously, if it is a sun-lover it requires a bright spot, and if it is partial to shade it needs a billet in the cool shadows. It is also important to give a plant room to grow. Find out its eventual height and spread, and position it accordingly; watch out for overhead wires and building foundations when planting trees and shrubs.

When you give plants – especially woody ones – the right amount of space for their needs, there may be large gaps while you are waiting for them to bulk out. You can fill in the voids with short-lived perennials or annuals, or plant ground-cover species that won't mind being

The sumach *Rhus typhina* 'Dissecta' has screaming crimson foliage in autumn.

edged out of the way as the larger plants expand. Suitable low-lying plants are bugle (*Ajuga reptans*), hardy geraniums, ivy (*Hedera* spp.), deadnettle (*Lamium maculatum*) and periwinkle (*Vinca* spp.). If a shrub or tree does outgrow its space, you may be able to prune it carefully into a more manageable size. But do try to keep the shape as graceful as possible by completely taking out some stems and shortening others. Avoid shaping shrubs into buns and giving trees Marine Corps haircuts, unless, of course, they are species that are traditionally maintained as clipped or pollarded specimens. Sometimes it is best to accept that the adult shrub or tree is taking up too much precious space, and it is time for it to move into the next phase of its life, as firewood or compost fodder.

GOING UP

Don't forget the walls of the garden: there are many plants that grow upwards, and that take up relatively little ground space. Climbers can disguise a run-of-the-mill panel fence, and make a small garden look larger by blurring its boundaries. They act as living wallpaper behind other plants, and offer a home for all manner of wildlife, including birds, which will build their nests

Ceanothus arboreus 'Trewithen Blue' is a good shrub for a south-facing wall. The deepest blue colour comes after cold winters.

in the thicker growth.

When you bring a climber home from the nursery or garden centre, it may be just a skinny little thing in its pot, a mere slip of a plant. Don't be deceived by this appearance of frailty: a couple of years down the line it may well have put on several kilos and acquired the physique of a rugby player. Although there are a few self-clinging climbers, most need a stout support: trellis, mesh or wire – depending on their growth habit. An adult climber can be surprisingly heavy, so when you are putting up supports, think of the weight of the foliage and stems, add the weight of the water from a bout of rain and, finally, add the force of the wind. When you are erecting trellis or wire mesh make sure that they are properly attached, so that they are not pulled down some stormy night. And if you are wiring a wall or fence for a twining plant, use sturdy wire, and proper vine-eyes to hold the wire: screw-in vine-eyes for timber and hammer-in ones for masonry.

Do put up the supporting structure before you put your climber into the ground, so that you can manoeuvre the shoots in the right direction from the start. Some plants, such as clematis, are impossible to retrain if they are allowed to head off on missions of their own. The stems snap when you try to coax them back from their wanderings, and the only thing to do is to prune them off and start anew. Clematis use their leaf stalks (the petioles) to hoist themselves up a framework and through adjacent plants. Other climbers use different methods to clamber upwards. Runner beans and wisteria have twining stems, while passion flowers and peas grasp with tendrils. Some plants are more leaners than climbers and may have to be tied in place with soft twine. When tying in new shoots of woody climbers, leaners or wall shrubs, loop the twine around the support first, knot it and then loosely tie in the shoot. Or use a loose figure-of-eight loop around the two. This gives the shoot room to expand, while ensuring that there is a layer of twine keeping it from rubbing against the support.

When you plant, remember that the soil at the base of walls is often dry, because of 'rain shadow', so put plenty of organic matter into the hole, and mulch the base of the plant to lock the moisture in.

All clematis ('Niobe' is shown here), climb with petioles or leaf stalks and need wire or another support to grab on to; *Solanum laciniatum* demands the warmest part of the garden, and may get felled by frost.

Warm walls – usually those that face south or west – offer a more clement microclimate, reflecting heat back on to the plants that they support. The extra warmth promotes flowering and fruiting, and also makes it possible to grow plants of questionable hardiness that might not survive elsewhere in the garden.

Colder walls may sit in the shade of buildings, or they may face north or east. The latter aspect can be treacherous to spring-flowering plants during frosty spells. The morning sun can quickly melt frozen blooms and shoots, making the cell walls burst and causing damage to these vulnerable parts. But there are many climbers that are used to living on the cool sides of mountains or in woodlands, and that are happy on cold walls in gardens.

Climbers and wall shrubs for a sunny and warm wall
- Californian lilac (*Ceanothus*): evergreen and deciduous wall shrubs, blue flowers
- *Dregea sinensis*: twiner with pink-marked white flowers, same family as the house plant *Hoya*
- *Solanum laxum* 'Album': white-flowered, semi-evergreen leaner and scrambler. *S. crispum* 'Glasnevin': purple-flowered, slightly hardier than *S. laxum*; may be too vigorous for small spaces
- Star jasmine (*Trachelospermum jasminoides*) and *T. asiaticum*: evergreen twiners with glossy leaves and starry white or cream flowers
- Passion flower (*Passiflora caerulea*): evergreen or semi-evergreen climber with lobed leaves and showy flowers

Climbers and wall shrubs for a shady, or part-shaded, cool wall

- Silk tassel bush (*Garrya elliptica*): evergreen wall shrub with long tasselled catkins in winter
- Ivies (*Hedera helix* and *H. colchica*): evergreen self-clingers, countless cultivars; those of the latter have big floppy leaves
- Climbing hydrangea (*Hydrangea anomala* subsp. *petiolaris*): self-clinging deciduous climber with white lace-cap clusters of flower
- Virginia creeper (*Parthenocissus quinquefolia*) and Boston ivy (*P. tricuspidata*): classic self-clinging climbers with beautiful autumn foliage; the related *P. henryana* has less spectacular autumn leaves and is less rampant
- *Rosa* 'Zéphirine Drouhin', a climbing Bourbon rose with deep pink fragrant flowers and no thorns; a good rose for a north wall, but prone to mildew, unfortunately

ANNUALS

These are the first plants that many of us grew as children – the hopeful sunflowers, the scrambling nasturtiums, the sweet sweet peas. They send a nostalgic glow straight to our adult gardening souls. And they're easy and quick: they flower and set seed all in the course of one year. Most produce blooms for many months. Almost all flowering annuals require a sunny patch in the garden, but a few, including busy lizzy (*Impatiens*), tobacco (*Nicotiana alata* and

Cornflowers (*Centaurea cyanus*) and opium poppy (*Papaver somniferum*) are easy annuals: the poppy will seed itself year after year.

N. sylvestris) and violas, will grow in shade. Most annuals are well supplied with nectar and pollen, and are much visited by insects. When choosing varieties, avoid those with double flowers (i.e. lots of additional petals), as the extra bulk in the bloom usually means that the nectar- and pollen-bearing parts are either absent or hard for insects to find.

Cornfield annuals have long, wiry stems, and can hold their own among naturalistic perennials and grasses. Dublin gardener Helen Dillon pops a few cornflowers (*Centaurea cyanus*) each year into her famous blue border, where they add to the smoky azure haze created by the agapanthus and *Verbena bonariensis*. Other similar European wild flowers that are gardenworthy include corncockle (*Agrostemma githago*), crown marigold (*Chrysanthemum coronarium*), corn marigold (*C. segetum*) and field poppy (*Papaver rhoeas*).

The English or pot marigold (*Calendula officinalis*), which has been used as a herb for centuries (hence the 'pot' in the name), is one of my favourite annuals – and it is much enjoyed by my local hoverflies and honeybees. Care must be taken when selecting a variety, as the modern ones are almost all doubles and of no use to pollen- and nectar-eaters. When you are choosing from a catalogue or from a selection of packets in a shop, check the picture to make sure that the central boss is clearly visible on the flower. There are hundreds of other annuals: their seed is inexpensive to buy, so they are a most expeditious way of filling up a new garden while you decide on more permanent planting.

Corncockle (*Agrostemma githago*) grows happily among meadow grasses and perennials, while English or pot marigold (*Calendula officinalis*) is a good nectar plant.

SELF-SEEDERS: THE GARDENER'S FRIEND (USUALLY)

Our garden is full of plants that seed themselves around year after year. Over time, their offspring march from one end of the garden to the other, hatched from seed carried on the wind, ferried in compost or bounced and skittered along the ground like miniature ball-bearings. Some seeds have hitchhiked on clothes or animal fur, while others have travelled through the innards of birds. Still others – such as those of the little blue wood violet, *Viola riviniana* – have been shot out of exploding pods to land up to 5 metres (16 feet) away. I love the dynamism of these plants: how they wander here and there, settling in communes, and maybe staying, or maybe upping and trekking further away.

Our front garden has been colonized by Corsican hellebore and stinking hellebore (*Helleborus argutifolius* and *H. foetidus*), which start to flower in late winter when little else is in bloom. And at the back of the house, there are gatherings of lofty Canary island echiums, ruby-petalled opium poppies, white foxgloves, teasels and many other bumptious volunteers. I treasure my self-seeders, and rely upon them to populate several areas in the garden. It is a lazy person's mode of gardening, but it is also a sure method of clothing the ground in a natural-looking way with robust plants that are perfectly suited to the soil, climate and aspect.

Gardening with so many self-seeders requires a ruthless streak: if you were to let every freelance seedling grow into an adult, the place would soon be overwhelmed by these species. Left unchecked, they would take over every patch of bare soil, and elbow out the more fragile

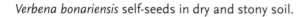

Verbena bonariensis self-seeds in dry and stony soil.

Primula beesiana seeds about in damp and heavy soil.

plants. In my garden, for each echium, teasel, foxglove and other self-invitee that reaches maturity, I cull dozens of their siblings. With some plants that are eager to spread their progeny, I remove most or all of the spent flower heads before the seeds ripen; lady's mantle (*Alchemilla mollis*) and hardy geraniums are two such plants that get the chop. This saves considerable time later on, as there are few or no seedlings. However, some plants (teasel, for example) have seed heads that are decorative, and that are beloved of birds, so I leave them intact, and resign myself to weeding out the unwanted youngsters in a few months' time. Needless to say, the seed (or any other part) of garden plants should never be introduced into the wild, as they offer unfair competition for native species.

A few valuable self-seeders

- Foxglove (*Digitalis purpurea*); the white form (*Digitalis purpurea* f. *albiflora)* is excellent for brightening dark corners
- The huge Canary Island echium (*E. pininana*) is hardy in most Irish gardens, and in more clement British ones; needs lean, dry soil
- Mexican fleabane (*Erigeron karvinskianus*) takes over crevices in paving and walls, and throws out clouds of tiny daisies
- Miss Willmott's ghost (*Eryngium giganteum*) is a silvery biennial sea holly
- Alpine strawberry (*Fragaria vesca*) is good for colonizing crevices along paths and steps
- Hardy geraniums are prolific self-seeders: *G. palmatum*, with cerise flowers and bristly pink stems, is one of the poshest
- Hellebores, including the Corsican hellebore (*Helleborus argutifolius*) and the stinking hellebore (*H. foetidus*), will grow in sun or shade
- Forget-me-not (*Myosotis sylvatica*) is a filler for gaps at the fronts of beds
- Evening primrose (*Oenothera stricta* 'Sulphurea') has large, pale-yellow, scented flowers that open at the end of the day
- Opium poppy (*Papaver somniferum*) has crêpe-paper petals and very decorative seed canisters
- Primulas self-replicate in moist soils
- *Verbascum* species have spires of blossom; *V. bombyciferum* and *V. olympicum* are woolly in stem and leaf and have pale yellow flowers
- *Verbena bonariensis* is an airy, purple-topped plant adored by bees and butterflies

BULBS THAT GO ON AND ON

Bulbous plants are perfect examples of nature's excellent design ability. The swollen underground structures of these geophytes (a catch-all term that incorporates corms, rhizomes and tubers as well as bulbs) contain stockpiles of food, laid down the previous season. The neat larders of carbohydrates, water and minerals allow the plants to survive a hot summer, or other adverse events, including browsing herbivores. Wild species generally return year after year in their natural habitats. But some garden bulbs are bred for a one-off festive bash, rather than for longevity. Big, showy tulips, for instance, are liable to disappear after a season or two, so if you want durability, it's better to call on less fussy varieties to do the job.

Tulips are classified into fifteen 'divisions', mainly according to their flowering periods and the shape of the blooms. Those in the Greigii, Kaufmanniana, Fosteriana and Darwin Hybrid divisions are more likely to rebloom. There are dozens to choose from, but the variety that I like, and which has faithfully rebloomed after several seasons in our garden, is 'Toronto', a Greigii kind. It produces two to three flowers per bulb, and has reddish-salmon petals, which perfectly complement the clenched-fist emerging foliage of peonies.

Other tulips that are likely to reappear annually – if they are planted where they get a good baking in summer, and where the bulbs do not rot in winter – are the so-called species or botanical tulips. These are wild species, or their natural derivations, that have been introduced by breeders. Some, such as the rosy-red 'Little Beauty', are no bigger than a crocus, while others, such the canary-coloured *T. sylvestris* and the pink and egg-yolk-yellow 'Lilac Wonder', are 30 centimetres (12 inches) or more tall.

The species tulips 'Lilac Wonder' and 'Little Beauty' may return year after year if the soil is well drained.

Aside from the one-off tulips, and some of the daffodils with big, complicated flowers, most bulbous plants will return to flower next year – if all goes well. That 'if' includes not being eaten by rodents, larvae, slugs or eelworm; not being guillotined by spades; not succumbing to a virus; not being attacked by fungal rot, or not otherwise turning up their toes and dying. If you like a certain kind of bulb, try a few of them out, and if they are happy, get a few more. I love blue, starry camassias and checkered snake's-head fritillaries, but because they like moist and fertile soil, both have perished in my dry ground. Instead, I'm building up numbers of alliums, species tulips and other bulbs that don't mind our thin soil.

BULBS IN GRASS AND UNDER TREES

The best places to naturalize bulbs are often the more difficult spots in the garden: the wild parts around the boundaries, the dry ground under deciduous trees or an awkward slope that puts you in a bad mood when you have to drag the mower over it. Sprinklings and swathes of daffodils in lawns are delightful, to be sure, but do remember that you won't be able to cut the grass until after the leaves begin to die back – and that could be the end of May. The foliage feeds the bulb, bulking it up after all its hard work in the flowering department. If you have a very large garden, and can do without your bulb lawn while the plants regenerate below, well and good. Otherwise, if you want bulbs in the lawn, plant them in a group (or groups, depending on how much space you have) and, when you need to cut the grass, mow gracefully around them so that they are left to grow in a nicely shaped island of long grass.

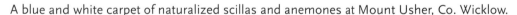

A blue and white carpet of naturalized scillas and anemones at Mount Usher, Co. Wicklow.

Bulbous plants to naturalize in grass and around deciduous trees

- *Allium sphaerocephalon*
- *Anemone blanda*, *A. nemorosa* and *A. apennina*
- *Camassia cusickii* and *C. leichtlinii*
- *Crocus tommasinianus* and other small crocuses, and the Dutch crocus (*C. vernus*)
- *Cyclamen hederifolium* (late summer and autumn)
- Winter aconite (*Eranthis hyemalis*)
- Dog's-tooth violet (*Erythronium dens-canis*)
- Snake's-head fritillary (*Fritillaria meleagris*)
- Snowdrop (*Galanthus* spp.)
- English bluebell (*Hyacinthoides non-scripta*)
- Spring snowflake (*Leucojum vernum*)
- Daffodils, many kinds, but the smaller and more wild-looking ones are best, including *Narcissus* 'Actaea', *N. cyclamineus*, *N. obvallaris*, *N. poeticus* var. *recurvus* and *N. pseudonarcissus*
- Star of Bethlehem (*Ornithogalum umbellatum*) and *O. nutans*
- Small squills, including *Scilla bifolia* and *S. siberica*

THE GARDEN WITH FERTILE, MOIST, WELL-DRAINED, LOAMY SOIL

This is the garden of which we all dream, but which only the blessed few have. This versatile soil allows almost any kind of plant to grow. It is the soil that is best for flowering perennials, especially all the beautiful American prairie plants such as echinacea and eupatorium, and the old-fashioned border perennials such as phlox and delphinium. Stately grasses, the likes of the *Miscanthus* tribe, grow thick and tall here; woodland plants thrive in shady spots; and plants from drier regions are often happy in the sunny areas. Princely garden plants such as clematis and roses are in their element; and fruit trees, fruit bushes and vegetables crop contentedly. If you have this kind of soil, you can pick from nearly everywhere on the plant menu to fill it.

THE DRY GARDEN

A dry garden in Ireland or Britain is a lush place, compared to the arid regions of California or Arizona. But on our green Atlantic islands anything under 750 millimetres (about 30 inches) of rainfall per year is at the low end of the scale. Add in sandy, light, free-draining soil that retains little water or nutrition and you have a patch that needs special treatment and careful planting. Garden compost – in the planting hole and used as a mulch – helps to feed the soil and increase its ability to retain moisture. Mulches should always be laid on ground that is weed free and damp. If you mulch soil when it is dry, it stays dry, as the moisture is locked out.

A plant's leaves will tell you if it is suitable for a dry garden. Foliage on drought-resistant plants is adapted in many ways. Furry or silky leaves (as on verbascum and lamb's ears) are insulated against extremes of temperature, and reflect the sun's rays with their hairy surfaces – as do blue-tinged or grey leaves. Plants with small, hard and thin leaves (rosemary, *Callistemon*) or feathery ones (fennel, cosmos) or with leathery or waxy coatings (bergenia, griselinia) are

Fritillaries and narcissus naturalized at Kilmacurragh Botanic Gardens in Co. Wicklow.

also able to survive dry soil. Some plants are like vegetable camels, storing water in their fat, succulent leaves (echeveria, sedum), allowing them to go for long periods without a drink.

When choosing individual plants, especially shrubs and trees, go for younger specimens. They will establish more readily than mature ones, which may receive a rude shock after a moisture-and nutrient-rich life in the nursery. Don't mind that the younger ones are smaller: they will catch up fast. There are hundreds of exciting plants for a dry garden, so it is hard to suggest only a few of my favourites.

Outdoor bulbs indoors
Some bulbs don't mind being dug up from the garden temporarily and brought into the house to bloom. Replant them as soon as they have faded, and give them a little garden compost or some blood-fish-and-bone to help them get over the trauma. Superstitious folk don't bring cut snowdrops indoors, as it is supposed to cause a death in the house, but apparently it is safe to grow them inside in a pot or bowl.

Allium cristophii, with football-sized spheres, does well in dry soil.

Perennials and grasses

- Globe thistle (*Echinops ritro*): silvery-blue ping-pong balls of flower with felt-backed, softly prickly leaves, 90cm (36in)
- The *Euphorbia* or spurge genus: countless perennial species, from the low 20cm (8in) and somewhat invasive (be careful where you put it) *E. cyparissias* 'Fens Ruby' to the muscular 1m (39in) *E. characias* subsp. *wulfenii* (the milky sap of spurges is an irritant: keep away from sensitive skin and eyes)
- *Phlomis russeliana*: heart-shaped leaves and yellow whorls of flower on tall stems, good winter skeletons, 90cm (36in)
- *Stipa*: grasses with greyish foliage and very good seed heads, including the fountain-like *S. gigantea* with light-catching golden awns, 2.5m (8ft); and *S. tenuissima*, the aptly named ponytail grass, 60cm (24in)
- Verbenas: slim, bony plants with blue, purple or pink flowers, including *V. bonariensis*, 1–2m (39–78in), *V. hastata*, 1–1.5m (39–60in); and *V. rigida*, 30–60cm (12–24in)
- Herbs: almost all are drought tolerant
- Succulents, including *Echeveria*, *Lampranthus spectabilis*, *Sedum* and houseleek (*Sempervivum*)

Bulbs

- *Allium*: there are dozens of ornamental onions, including *A. cristophii*, which bears shiny lavender-coloured orbs as big as a football
- Most daffodils and species tulips are fairly happy in a dry garden
- Some snowdrops struggle, but *Galanthus elwesii*, from Turkey, is suitable

Shrubs and trees

- Mimosa (*Acacia dealbata*): delicate, ferny leaved tree, with tiny pom-poms of pale yellow blossom from winter to early summer, needs shelter from wind, 5–30m (16–100ft)
- Rock roses (*Cistus*): evergreen shrubs with papery flowers in many varieties and colours, from 30cm (12in) to 2m (6½ft)
- *Ceanothus*: known as Californian lilac, for its miniature lilac-style clusters of blue blossom, many varieties, from dwarf to very large shrubs, several metres tall

Stipa gigantea looks like golden rain when backlit by the evening sun, while *Phlomis russeliana* has a pleasing structure, both alive and dead (see page 183).

- *Cordyline australis*, New Zealand cabbage palm: the 'palm tree' admired by tourists to Ireland and the warmer parts of Britain, up to 10m (33ft)
- *Cotinus coggygria*: the smoke bush, with puffs of flower borne in summer among oval leaves; the species has greeny-blue leaves; 'Grace' and 'Royal Purple' have maroon leaves; will grow several metres tall, but can be drastically pruned in spring
- *Eucalyptus*: the gum trees, from 6m (20ft) to near infinity
- *Perovskia atriplicifolia* 'Blue Spires': short-lived, angular, shrubby character with grey-green leaves and lavender-esque flowers, dislikes being crowded, 1.2m (4ft)
- Pine, cedar, cypress and holly are also suitable

Show-off plants
- *Agave*: fabulously spiny succulent, can stand only a degree or two of frost without protection, usually up to 75cm (30in) in Ireland and Britain
- Artichokes and cardoons: grey, felted, angularly cut foliage and mauve-tipped flowers, 2–3m (6½–10ft)
- Echiums: *E. pininana*, coarse foliage and a rocket of blue bloom, up to 3m (10ft); *E. candicans* (pride of Madeira), shrubby with grey foliage and many blue, pinkish or mauve frothy spikes, 2m (6½ft); *E. wildpretii*, grey, felt-covered leaves and a single elongated nosecone of red flowers, 2–3m (6½–10ft)
- *Verbascum bombyciferum* and *V. olympicum*: huge woolly spires of yellow flowers, up to 2m (6½ft)

Japanese anemones, such as 'Prinz Heinrich', bring light to shady corners.

DRY SHADE

Dry shade can occur in any garden, under trees or in the shadow of a building. Plants that grow here are often tough self-preservationists, quick to spread by seed or by creeping through the soil. When you plant them first, water them well, and keep an eye on them during dry periods in their first season.

Durable plants for dry shade

- Pheasant's tail grass (*Anemanthele lessoniana*): arching evergreen, olive-coloured grass, turns reddish in autumn, 60cm (24in)
- Japanese anemone (*Anemone × hybrida* and *A. hupehensis*): pink or white flowers on wiry stems, 50–120cm (20–48in)
- *Bergenia*: sometimes endearingly known as elephant's ears, with large, leathery leaves and sprays of white or pink flowers 35–60cm (14–24in)
- *Euphorbia amygdaloides* var. *robbiae*: evergreen spurge with dark green leaves and lime flowers, a terrific runner, so don't let it loose elsewhere, 70cm (28in)
- *Geranium macrorrhizum*: hardy geranium, semi-evergreen, sticky, resin-scented foliage, white or pink flowers, depending on the variety, 40cm (16in)
- Solomon's seal (*Polygonatum × hybridum*): arching stems with elongated green-tipped pearls of flowers, 120cm (48in)
- Ferns: the male fern (*Dryopteris filix-mas*) and hart's-tongue fern (*Asplenium scolopendrium*)

THE MOIST GARDEN

A damp garden might have heavy clay soil that is wet in winter and baked in dry weather; or it might be boggy, waterlogged ground; or it could be a shady area that doesn't get much sun. Or it may well be a combination of all or some of the above. Whichever it is, you must choose plants that are tolerant of some degree of moisture at their roots. *Beth Chatto's Damp Garden* goes into all aspects of the subject in detail, and is the best book I know for gardeners with moist soil.

Iris ensata, arum lily (*Zantedeschia aethiopica*), primulas and meadowsweet (*Filipendula* sp.) saturate this damp hollow with colour at the Bay Garden in Co. Wexford.

Soil that retains plenty of moisture favours plants with big, sumptuous leaves, such as skunk cabbage, arum lilies, ligularia and many others. The homelands of these species are diverse: the damp mountain meadows of central Europe, the streamsides of Japan, the river banks of North America. If you have this kind of soil you can have a luxuriant and jungly garden that looks as if it stepped out of a painting by Henri '*Le Douanier*' Rousseau. The French naive artist, famous for his primitive and stylized depictions of exuberant vegetation during the late nineteenth and early twentieth centuries, never actually left Paris, and based his tropical landscapes on plants observed in the glasshouses at the city's Jardin des Plantes.

The big-leaved damp-dwelling species have strong root systems, and will quickly form a weed-stifling blanket of greenery. Less vigorous plants may also be smothered, so mind where you put the more dainty moisture-lovers, such as primulas. Woodland plants from deciduous forests are also at ease in the shadier parts of a garden with moist soil. There are innumerable plants that flourish in damp or merely moist places. Those listed below are just a handful.

Perennials with striking foliage that thrive in permanently damp soil

- Umbrella plant (*Darmera peltata*): pink drumsticks of flowers, followed by parasol-like leaves, which may expand to 60cm (24in) across, height up to 1m (39in)
- *Iris ensata*: showy moisture-loving irises from Japan and eastern Asia with white, pink, lavender or purple flowers, 90cm (36in)
- Yellow flag (*Iris pseudacorus*): the native yellow iris, 90cm (36in)
- Skunk cabbage (*Lysichiton*): *L. americanus* has yellow spathes (cowl-like floral structures), and huge leaves later on, up to 1m (39in) long; *L. camtschatcensis* is about half the size, with white spathes
- Shuttlecock fern (*Matteuccia struthiopteris*): lime-green fronds that catch the spring light most beauteously; dislikes full sun; grows to 1.5m (5ft)
- Arum lily (*Zantedeschia aethiopica*): the 'Easter lily' of Ireland commemorates the Easter Rising of 1916, broad arrow-shaped leaves and white semi-furled flowers, 1.2m (4ft)

Other perennials for moist soil

- Meadowsweet (*Filipendula*): *F. ulmaria* is our native meadowsweet, bearing clouds of ivory flowers heavily fragrant with the smell of the countryside; others include the pink-puffed *F. purpurea*, 1–1.2m (39–48in); and *F. rubra* 'Venusta', 2–2.5m (7–8ft)
- Hostas: hundreds of cultivars, the smallest have teaspoon-sized foliage, the largest have leaves as big as paddles, most are beloved of slugs, but those with blueish foliage are said to be less tasty

Shuttlecock fern (*Matteuccia struthiopteris*) shows off its filigreed fronds in low sunlight.

- Purple loosestrife (*Lythrum*): *L. salicaria* and *L. virgatum*, the former is native here, but is highly invasive in the USA, muscling out indigenous plant species, and threatening waterfowl habitats by filling in tracts of open water; it is perfectly safe to plant in the UK and Ireland, though. Many varieties of both species exist, 80–120cm (32–48in)
- *Primula*: many kinds, from the ground-hugging native primrose (*P. vulgaris*), 6in (30cm), to the towering Himalayan cowslip (*P. florindae*), 35–100cm (14–39in)
- Globe flower (*Trollius*): elegant members of the buttercup family, with eye-catching yellow blooms, 60–90cm (24–36in)

A few woodlanders for moist soil in semi-shade

- *Actaea*, formerly known as *Cimicifuga*: varieties include black snakeroot or black cohosh (*A. racemosa*), which is used in menopause preparations, and bugbane (*A. simplex*); the Atropurpurea Group has bronzy stems and leaves; 1–2m (39–78in)
- Bleeding heart (*Dicentra*): arching stems and delicately trembling heart-shaped lockets of flowers; several species and cultivars; the pink-and-white *D. spectabilis* is the showiest 1.2m (4ft)
- Lilies: many, including *Lilium martagon*, 1.2m (4ft) and the splendiferous giant *Cardiocrinum giganteum*, up to 4m (13ft)
- *Uvularia grandiflora*: graceful, spring flowering American with pendant yellow flowers and foliage that remains fresh all summer, 45cm (18in)

Native yellow flag (*Iris pseudacorus*) will grow with its feet in water. *Uvularia grandiflora* is a choice North American woodlander.

Katsura (*Cercidiphyllum japonicum*) has warm autumn colour and a tantalizing smell of burnt sugar that wafts gently on the air.

Trees and shrubs
- Alder (*Alnus*): *A. glutinosa* is the native alder, and there are many others, 6–25m (20–80ft)
- Katsura (*Cercidiphyllum japonicum*): tree with heart-shaped leaves; autumn colour is best on acid soil; 8–10m (25–33ft)
- Dogwood (*Cornus*): a versatile genus with many excellent shrubs and trees, some with showy bracts on their inflorescences; cultivars of *C. alba*, *C. sanguinea* and *C. sericea* can be pruned right back to the base every year or two for showy stems
- *Hydrangea macrophylla* and *H. paniculata*: classic shrubs with dozens of varieties available; *H. paniculata* 'Limelight' has clusters of lime green flowers that fade to yellow and then pink; 3m (10ft)
- Willow (*Salix*): large group of excellent trees and shrubs; most don't mind waterlogged soil; cultivars of *S. alba* can be pruned hard in spring, in the same way as dogwoods; keep large trees away from buildings as roots may be troublesome
- Swamp cypress (*Taxodium distichum*), birch, silver fir (*Abies alba*) and *Thuja occidentalis* are also suitable

PLANTS FOR PONDS
Yellow flag and arum lily (see above) will grow with their feet in a few centimetres of water, as will the flowering rush (*Butomus umbellatus*) and bulrushes (*Typha*); but be careful, as all can be rampant, and can overwhelm a small pool. For deeper water, aquatic plants are required, but again, caution is important. Water plants from garden ponds have colonized lakes and waterways, choking them and affecting native species. At the time of writing, legislation in Ireland is pending to ban the following non-native aquatic plants: curly-leaved pondweed (*Lagarosiphon major*), fairy fern (*Azolla filiculoides*), New Zealand pygmy weed (*Crassula helmsii*), Nuttall's pondweed (*Elodea nuttallii*), parrot's feather (*Myriophyllum aquaticum*) and fringed water lily (*Nymphoides peltata*). All these, and floating pennywort (*Hydrocotyle ranunculoides*), are likely to be banned also in the UK.

Water lilies (*Nymphaea*) are quite safe and beautiful, as are native aquatic plants. Among these are the oxygenating plants, spiked water milfoil (*Myriophyllum spicatum*), whorled water milfoil (*M. verticillatum*) and curled pondweed (*Potamogeton crispus*). Even if you buy plants that bear the above names, don't think of disposing of extra bits anywhere except for the compost heap. It's possible that they may have been mislabelled and are actually the invasive foreigners.

THE SEASIDE GARDEN

Coastal gardens are delightful when all is calm. At other times, however, they can get a serious battering from the weather. The wind rocks and shreds plants, and blows them dry. The salt on the breeze doesn't help either: it too has a desiccating effect, sucking moisture out of plant tissues. The light by the sea is intense, with sunlight reflected off the water, and with little shade providing relief. Coastal soil is sandy, free draining and lacking both moisture and nutrition. Only lean, mean plants can survive here: those that are adapted to withstand the harsh weather and light, the scarcity of food and water, and a shifting, unstable footing. Their leaves are modified to cope with the high light and the dehydrating conditions. Their underground parts are also specialized, and may be either taprooted (as in sea holly) or extensively spreading (lyme grass). Both of these root configurations serve to stabilize the plants, and to seek out water, by drilling deep or by questing far and wide.

The seaside environment presents a challenge, but it has one distinct advantage: the sea acts as a moderating influence on temperatures, so frost is very rare. Coastal gardeners are able to grow plants that their inland friends must keep tucked up in a south-facing courtyard or in a glasshouse.

Sunny balconies, incidentally, are a bit like being at the seaside: they are subject to drying winds, and to high light conditions. So if you live in an apartment with a south-facing terrace or balcony, imagine that you are overlooking the seashore, and plant accordingly.

Shelter is the first thing that you must think of with a coastal garden. There are a number of stalwart, sea-friendly trees and shrubs that are able to filter the wind and catch the salt, and act as your first line of defence. Depending on how windy the area is, several layers of shelter-belt planting may be required. Use small, young plants, so that they can build up strong root systems to cope with the wind. You may need to erect a temporary barrier of windbreak netting to give them a chance to establish. Even so, expect some casualties: life on the edge of the sea is stormy and eventful.

Trees suitable for shelter planting include alder, strawberry tree (*Arbutus unedo*), hawthorn (*Crataegus*), European black pine (*Pinus nigra*), white poplar (*Populus alba*) and evergreen oak (*Quercus ilex*). For shrubs fit for maritime planting, see pages 62–3. Additional seaside-worthy woody specimens include *Elaeagnus* × *ebbingei*, Japanese spindle (*Euonymus japonicus*), tamarisk (*Tamarix tetrandra*) and sea buckthorn (*Hippophae rhamnoides*). Do not plant this last if your garden is near an area of pristine coastland, as it can spread and edge out native species.

Most of the species that I recommended for the dry garden (see pages 78–9) are also suitable for a coastal garden, as long as they have a bit of protection from the worst of the gales. Likewise, all the plants suggested for the seaside will also thrive in a dry garden.

Plants for the seaside garden (some need a little shelter)

* African lily (*Agapanthus*): regal plants with blue (sometimes white) spherical clusters of tubular flowers and long strappy leaves 45–150cm (18–60in)

Sea pink (*Armeria maritima*) and seakale (*Crambe maritima*) are two natives that are comfortable in both seaside and dry gardens.

- Sea pink (*Armeria maritima*): native plant with pink flowers borne on pincushions of grassy foliage; several cultivars are available; 15–40cm (6–16in)
- Cupid's dart (*Catananche caerulea*): short-lived perennial with bobbing blue papery flowers on wiry stems, 60–90cm (24–36in)
- Seakale (*Crambe maritima*): glorious native with large, undulating, blue-grey leaves and sprays of sweetly scented white flowers; the emerging foliage is beautifully engorged with purple; 40–90cm (16–36in)
- Sea hollies (*Eryngium*): annuals, biennials and perennials with silvery foliage, and cone-shaped flowers surrounded by spiny silver or metallic blue bracts, adored by nectar-supping insects, from about 50cm–150cm (20–60in)
- Red hot poker (*Kniphofia*): orange, terracotta or yellow torches and messy, strappy leaves; makes a stirring picture when planted en masse; many varieties, from the petite 'Little Maid' 45cm (18in) to the massive 3m (10ft) *K. uvaria* 'Nobilis'
- South African restios: grass-like plants of many shapes and sizes; signature plants of posh Cork gardeners

SCENT IN THE GARDEN: THAT SMELL REMINDS ME OF . . .

Whenever I smell lily-of-the-valley, I am carried back more than forty years to the shady back garden of a house in Minnesota, where I lived as a very small child. Scent has a physiological relationship with nostalgia. Our olfactory receptors send nerve impulses straight to the limbic system, the part of the brain that deals with emotion and memories. This means, in effect, that smells zoom past the mental speed bumps and traffic controls monitored by the departments of logic and analysis, and crash straight into the heart of the brain. So even if an agreeable fragrance doesn't trigger a memory, it can stimulate an almost feral bout of exhilaration.

Although sweetly scented blooms send the human nose into ecstasies, their odour is directed towards the insects that pollinate them. Without the ability to get up and go looking for a mate, plants must dupe creatures into carrying their pollen to another flower. Some flowers mimic the female pheromones of certain insects, while others just smell like food. Winter-blooming plants are often highly scented because they have to send out a stronger signal to summon the few pollinators that are out and about in cold weather.

Scented plants deserve a special position in the garden: by a door or window, or near a sitting area. Or put them by your gate, where they will pleasantly ambush passers-by. One of the sweetest of all summer flowers is night-scented stock (*Matthiola longipetala* subsp. *bicornis*), a self-effacing annual with mauvy-pink flowers that wilt during the day. It is traditional to grow it with the similar-looking Virginia stock (*Malcolmia maritima*), which has no scent, but which doesn't suffer from daytime bashfulness. When the afternoon fades, night-scented stock unfurls its cruciform flowers and pours out its sugary perfume, a heady mixture of coconut and cloves. When you sow the seed, include a pot to bring into your bedroom at night, or to place on the windowsill outside, so that it can waft through your dreams.

There are scented flowers for every season, so you can have good smells drifting through the air at all times of the year.

Winter
Camellia; wintersweet (*Chimonanthes praecox*); *Daphne* including *D. bholua* 'Jacqueline Postill' and 'Gurkha', *D. odora*, *D. blagayana*; witch hazel (*Hamamelis* 'Pallida' is supposed to be the most fragrant); *Mahonia*; paperwhites (*Narcissus papyraceus*, for indoors); Christmas box (*Sarcococca confusa* and *S. hookeriana*); *Viburnum* × *bodnantense* 'Dawn'.

Spring
Chocolate vine (*Akebia quinata*), *Clematis armandii*, *Azalea*, lily-of-the-valley (*Convallaria majalis*); wallflower (*Erysimum cheiri*); honey spurge (*Euphorbia mellifera*); *Narcissus poeticus* and *N. jonquilla* cultivars; mock orange (*Philadelphus* 'Belle Étoile' is highly scented).

Summer
Various clematis; chocolate cosmos (*C. atrosanguineus*); pinks and carnations (*Dianthus*); heliotrope or cherry pie (*Heliotropium arborescens*); jasmine; lavender; lilies; honeysuckle (*Lonicera*); night-scented stock (*Matthiola longipetala* subsp. *bicornis*); tobacco (*Nicotiana alata* and *N. sylvestris*); roses; sweet pea.

Autumn
Abelia × *grandiflora*; various clematis; *Magnolia grandiflora*; California tree poppy (*Romneya coulteri*), roses.

Latin names: a *sine qua non* for defining plants

When you're starting out to garden, or if you're just a casual dabbler, 'serious' gardeners who bandy about Latin names can seem like members of an exclusive and pretentious club. But, despite its tiresome ostentation, botanical Latin is a perfect tool for defining plants. It allows gardeners and plant people to communicate quickly and efficiently, pinning down a plant precisely, so that there is no doubt about its identity. Common names are fine when we're all speaking the same vernacular, but if not, problems can arise.

For instance, my sister, who lives in America, was complaining that some villain had killed her 'myrtle'. Living in Ireland, I know myrtle as an evergreen tree with foamy white blossom and interesting orange patchworky bark (*Luma apiculata*) – far too tender, I would have thought, to survive in Massachusetts. 'No! No! No!' barks the sister, who refuses to entertain Latin names. 'You know, *myrtle*, the traily thing that lies on the ground, with little blue flowers!' 'Ah, periwinkle!' I say, uttering the common name that is used on this side of the Atlantic, and then risk annoying her with its Latin name: '*Vinca*?'

And indeed, *Vinca* it was, although what particular species or variety is still a mystery. Often, common names – even when they are understood – are unable to unambiguously describe the exact identity of a plant. Some plants, indeed the majority, do not have widely known common names. So it makes sense for one gardener to say to another: 'Can I have a bit of your *Silphium perfoliatum*?' instead of 'I'd love to have some of that really tall yellow daisy with the big floppy dark green leaves – no, no, no, not the sunflower, the other one . . .'

Carl Linnaeus, in his 1753 book *Species Plantarum*, laid out the system that we still use for naming plants: every newly named plant must conform to these rules. The Swedish naturalist gathered plants into families, bringing together those that had certain similarities in their flowers, fruits and other parts. Within each family, he nominated smaller, more closely related clusters, called genera (which is the plural of genus). And in each genus he placed individual species. In this splendid binomial system, every plant is identified by a unique and universal two-part name: the genus, followed by the 'specific epithet', a one-word description that distinguishes a particular species from others within the genus. So we have *Vinca minor* and *Vinca major*, two distinct species of periwinkle (or myrtle, if you must), one with small flowers and the other with large. *Vinca* is the genus name, while *minor* and *major* denote the different species within it. Some plant species are further divided into subspecies, varieties, forms and cultivars, to denote variations from the norm: *Vinca minor* f. *alba*, for example, has white flowers, instead of the usual blue.

Specific epithets may indicate size (as in *minor* and *major*), shape (*pyramidalis*), colour (*violaceus*), place of origin (*hispanicus*) or other attribute (*hirsutus*, *gracilis*,

One of many myrtles, the Chilean tree known as *Luma apiculata*, and, not just any tall yellow daisy, but *Silphium perfoliatum*.

luxurians, etc.). Or they may commemorate a person or event; or they might just be a bit of fun, as in the case of *Kalanchoe mitejea*, where *mitejea* is an anagram of *je t'aime*.

Genus names may derive from Greek or classical Latin: *Vinca* comes in a roundabout way from *vincio*, meaning 'to bind', because the stems of periwinkle were used to make wreaths. The names may also honour people, as in the engaging *Captaincookia*, an endangered plant from New Caledonia; or places, as in the anagrammatical *Lobivia*, a cactus from Bolivia. Or they might be thoroughly whimsical creations, such as the orchid genus *Aa*, which guarantees it first place in an alphabetical list.

When talking about plants, I use the common name if possible, but there are many cases where Latin is the only accurate way to describe a particular plant. Having said that, I have no patience with gardeners who use botanical Latin to convey self-importance, rather than in the pursuit of greater clarity. I feel like smacking them with a trowel when they bellow '*Taraxacum officinale*' when all they mean is dandelion.

CREATURES: THE GARDEN POPULATION

'I once had a sparrow alight upon my shoulder for a moment, while I was hoeing in a village garden, and I felt that I was more distinguished by that circumstance than I should have been by any epaulet I could have worn.'
Henry David Thoreau, *Walden*

You will find creatures flying, crawling and hopping all over this book – in the same way that they do in a healthy garden – but I want to concentrate on them a little more in this chapter.

On a good week, when weather and time allow, I spend thirty or more hours in the garden – working, photographing, eating, communing with the hens, studying tadpoles, admiring sparrows, just using any excuse not to be indoors. At times like these, I feel bonded with nature and elated. Yet, when I think about it, that amount of time is paltry. In reality, I'm only a visitor to the garden. The robin that follows me around when I'm weeding, the burly spiders that drape their Hammer Horror cobwebs in the compost enclosure, the snail that pokes its eggs into my auricula pots: these are the true citizens. They don't leave when it gets a bit chilly, or if there is something good on television. It is their garden more than mine, so I try to let them get on with it (within reason, that is – more on those snails later).

This is not just benign guardianship on my part. The animals that inhabit our outdoor spaces are as crucial to life on this planet as the air we breathe. From the most minuscule and basic soil microbe to the highly evolved robin – with its millions of cells and thousands of moving parts – they all have a role to play. For example, if there were no creatures living in the soil, the ground below us would be dead, incapable of processing the organic materials that nature drops on to it, and that we, as gardeners, give it in the form of compost and manure. It is almost entirely thanks to the labours of its umpteen million tiny workers that soil is able to manufacture food for plants.

Above ground too, balance is maintained by an interdependent community of creatures. The most obvious relationship between them is that where those lower down on the food chain end up in the bellies of those above. The aphid is breakfast for the spider that is lunch for the baby blackbird that is dinner for the magpie that becomes a midnight feast for the fox. This concentric schedule of lower-downs being eaten by higher-ups is just another manifestation of the web of life – although to those involved there is a world of difference between eating and being eaten. Still, all this activity is a very good thing. Varieties of species – both visible and

A baby sparrow sits on a viburnum, waiting for its parents to come back and feed it.

invisible – increase in congenial gardens where there is adequate food, and add another layer of wildlife, making a more diverse and healthy ecosystem. In a plot that is teeming with wild things, plagues of pests are less likely to occur. Aphids become food for predatory insects and birds, and slugs and snails are eaten by ground beetles, thrushes and frogs.

Some relationships between creatures are stranger than the simple one of someone becoming someone else's dinner. Aphids, for instance, are frequently 'farmed' by ants. The ants carry the aphids to particularly succulent plants, and then collect the sugary liquid that the miniature herds excrete. (This waste plant sap is known as honeydew.) The ants 'milk' the aphids by stroking and patting their torsos with their antennae. In our garden, every year the industrious drovers wrangle black aphids on to the artichokes, and fight off the opportunistic ladybirds that drop by, hoping to pick up a plump aphid for a snack. The ants are no match for the blue tits, though, who find rich pickings here for their young in early summer. Ants are not alone in feeding off the produce of aphids' backsides: butterflies – both speckled wood and holly blue – are also dependent on honeydew.

Animals interact with plants also in more complex ways than just consuming them. Flowers produce nectar as a reward for insects, which unwittingly transport pollen to the stigma of the next flower from which they sup. Without pollinating insects there would be no fruits or seeds on the majority of our plants. (Members of the grass family and some trees are wind pollinated, but most plants rely on flying or crawling creatures to ferry their male gametes to a receptive female organ.)

Fruits, also, are part of the bargain that exists between plants and animals. The bird that has a lovely meal of alpine strawberries in my garden will excrete the seeds in the neighbours' patch, or in a lane 500 metres away, or somewhere else, where – with a bit of luck – the conditions are just right for a new strawberry plant. In the same way, nut-bearing shrubs and trees depend on animals hoarding their produce and neglecting to retrieve all of it. These reciprocal arrangements are known as mutualism, which is one of the things that keeps the millions of small cogs in nature's vast engine chugging along.

The gardener's friend, the robin, keeps a beady eye on the camera lens.

The collared dove: often to be seen with a mate, indulging in endearing displays of togetherness.

BIRDS OF THE AIR

Of all the animals that live in our gardens, birds are among the most engaging: few of them are destructive, most of them are helpful in keeping pest numbers down and their carry-on is like a human soap opera in miniature. Property disputes, bitter rivalries, frenetic courtships, sex (lots of it, and sometimes with a mixed bag of partners) and its consequences (babies, babies and more babies) are all part of the birdly daytime drama.

Birds will visit a garden if their basic needs are met, namely, shelter, food and water. They are most comfortable where the planting is arranged in layers, in the same formation as a woodland edge: trees are underplanted with shrubs and bordered by herbaceous plants and grass. This planting doesn't have to be extensive, and can be adapted to fit the smallest garden. A single tree (birch or rowan are very bird friendly) can be accompanied by a shrub or two and a handful of herbaceous perennials and ornamental grasses. Trees are important, not just because of the food and shelter that they offer, but also because they act as lookout posts from which to scour a terrain for danger or rivals. They are essential as song perches too, so that a bird can proclaim its territorial rights to a patch of land. If your garden is too small for a tree, or if you haven't planted one yet, you can provide a substitute in the shape of a bamboo or hazel wigwam, a home-made obelisk or simply a post banged into the ground with a sheaf of twigs tied

A baby blackbird, just a day out of its nest, sitting quietly in a shrub.

to it. In our garden, when teasel or artichoke seed heads are knocked by the wind we attach them to a pole near the bird table, so that the feathered troupes have somewhere to congregate midway between the wall shrubs and the feeding station.

Dense shrubs, hedges and climbers present prime real-estate opportunities for nest building. Certain birds, however, seem a bit dim about choosing a safe location – to my eyes, anyway. I cannot understand why blackbirds often construct their nests in full view of patrolling magpies. The stress of protecting eggs and babies must be mighty. Last year, I was astonished, however, to see a male blackbird go up to a too-inquisitive magpie and head-butt it, after which the female joined in and chased it away. Blackbirds: 1, magpies: 0.

Some birds will use nest boxes: the tit family, house sparrows, robins and wrens are among those who are happy to move into a man-made home. Site it in a safe, quiet place away from the bird table, at least 2 metres (6½ feet) from the ground. Face it between north and south-east, to avoid hot sunlight, and angle it slightly forward so that rain cannot enter. Boxes should be put up between autumn and winter so that they are in place when the house-hunting season starts in February. They should be cleaned out yearly, in mid-autumn. Remove all the old material, and scald the inside with boiling water, to kill parasites. Allow to dry before putting the lid back on. (Both Birdwatch Ireland and the RSPB have nest box plans on their websites: see Resources, page 204.)

The best kind of food that a gardener can provide for birds is the natural kind. Plants with berries and seed heads are important providers of sustenance. But so also are those that offer a home or hiding place for insects and other invertebrates, as these supply necessary protein for the avian diet. In wintertime, evergreen plants harbour small colonies of aphids, while the leaf litter on the soil surface is a rich hunting ground for woodlice, springtails and other detritivores – as well as the spiders and beetles that dine on them.

Water should be available at all seasons, for drinking and for bathing. Birds need to keep their feathers in good order, and shimmying in water (and dust) is part of their elaborate preening routine. You don't need to supply a garden pond or a fancy bird bath: a shallow, heavy container, such as a large plant saucer, is perfectly adequate. Birds, especially young

This blue tit may look fat, but its girth is merely its puffed-up feathers, a defence against the cold. A baby great tit sits in a birch tree.

ones, can drown in uncovered water barrels, so do fit them with a grid or a cover. I learned this the hard way when I found a very dead baby blackbird floating in the water butt outside the greenhouse.

THE BIRD CAFÉ

We feed the birds all year round in our garden, but we are especially conscientious in the winter. As the season wears on, natural food stocks become scarcer and the weather grows harsher. Small birds are especially vulnerable in the cold, dark months when there is less daylight for feeding, and when the low temperatures cause their body fat to burn off quickly. Consider this: our common birds, the wren and the blue tit, weigh only 10 and 11 grams respectively, but on a cold night they often lose 10 per cent or more of their body weight. In particularly severe conditions, losses of over 20 per cent have been recorded. The goldcrest, our tiniest bird, weighs just 6 grams. (You could post eight of them anywhere in Ireland for the price of a first-class stamp. And in Britain, you get a far better deal, and could dispatch twice that number to any address within the UK.) Tiny birds have a large surface area in relation to their body mass, so keeping warm is a constant challenge. When they are cold, they fluff up their feathers, making them look fat and happy, but the reality is that they are under great pressure trying to stay alive.

With such rapid and dramatic weight fluctuations, death from hypothermia is a daily possibility in bitter weather. On frosty mornings, a nourishing feed first thing can make all the difference. Grated cheese (from those hard ends close to the rind) can be a life saver. We put it on the bird table, and scatter it on the ground, as some birds are happier foraging at soil level. Other kitchen leftovers that make nourishing bird food are brown bread, cake, scraps of fat and cooked pasta, rice, grains and potatoes. It's worth noting that refined foods such as white bread are not very nutritious, and should not be fed in quantity.

Also, in order to avoid attracting rats and mice, put out only small amounts of food, and don't do it last thing at night.

Windfall apples will bring in blackbirds and thrushes if you leave them on the ground. And if you slice them in half and impale them on a branch, blackcaps will come – if they are in the area.

We have one main food depot with a table and hanging feeders, but we also suspend nut and seed holders, and fat balls, from various trees so that the shyer birds don't have to compete with the hooligan house sparrows.

Domestic, stray and feral cats can be gruesomely destructive to populations of garden birds (and frogs too). Most kill for sport rather than for food. A well-loved moggy is quite capable of strolling outside after its dinner for a spot of recreational killing. Birds are most at risk just after dawn and before sunset, as these periods are the times when they are feeding most intensively. Accordingly, bird-feeding stations should be situated at least 2 metres (6½ feet) from places where cats can hide and spring out for an attack.

Poor hygiene on feeders can also lead to bird deaths. Diseases such as *E. coli* and salmonella can be passed on through infected droppings. Bird feeders and tables should be regularly

The fieldfare, one of our regular winter visitors, tucks into some apple.

Native spindle bush (*Euonymus europaeus*): the shocking pink capsules contain orange berries, much liked by birds.

scrubbed with a 10 per cent bleach solution, and stale food and seed hulls should be removed from the ground. Another source of concern is aflatoxin, a poison produced by some *Aspergillus* fungi. It can occur in grains and nuts that have been stored in humid conditions, or that become overly damp. Peanuts are more likely to be affected than other foods. It is now possible to buy aflatoxin-free peanuts – but they should still be carefully stored and used up quickly. All seeds and other bird feeds should be kept in a cool dry place, preferably in sealed containers to avoid attention from mice, moths, weevils and other unsavoury characters.

But remember, as important as it is to provide extra food for birds, especially in hard weather, the thing that brings them in – and makes them stay – is a welcoming habitat. The songbird that is flying over a row of back gardens will have its interest more piqued by a patch of leafy shelter (and the promise of what lies within) than by a designer bird table sitting in the middle of a pristine patio. Our garden played host to only a few bird species when I moved here twenty years ago. Now there are over three dozen that stop by regularly – which is not bad for a town plot. If you plant for them, they will come.

FOR THE BIRDS
Berrying trees, shrubs and climbers
There are many fruiting trees that attract birds. Here are a few of the more readily available ones. Red fruits are usually eaten first, then orange and finally yellow. All the berriers mentioned are first-class nectar plants also – so are excellent for bees.

Shrubs and climbers
Cotoneaster horizontalis and *C. frigidus* 'Cornubia' are good wall shrubs, as are most *Pyracantha* cultivars. If you have a bit more room, try these natives: guelder rose (*Viburnum opulus*), spindle (*Euonymus europaeus*) and holly (*Ilex aquifolium*). Most hollies are either one sex or the other, so you need one of each to get berries. However, the cultivar *I. aquifolium* 'J.C. van Tol' is

self-fertile, and makes its berries all by itself. The rugosa rose (*Rosa rugosa*) can be planted as an informal hedge, offering safe nesting and roosting spots, and huge, important-looking and tasty (if you're a bird) hips. Ivy (*Hedera helix*) produces black fruits that are popular with woodpigeons, starlings, thrushes and blackcaps. Its waterproof evergreen leaves make it a sterling shelter plant.

Trees

Our native rowan or mountain ash (*Sorbus aucuparia*) earns its specific epithet from the Latin *aucupor*, meaning 'to catch birds'. As its name suggests, it is a magnet for fruit-eaters: in some years rowans in suburban areas are visited by dapper-looking waxwings, which travel down en masse from northern Europe when their local foods become scarce. The Asian mountain rowans, *S. commixta* and *S. sargentiana*, are also fine berry-bearers. Crab apples (*Malus*) offer splendid avian fuel: 'Golden Hornet' has beautiful yellow fruits, 'Red Sentinel' and 'Profusion' both carry red orbs (the latter has dark pink flowers in spring) and 'John Downie' is hung with elongated tiny orange apples – supposedly the best for preserves (if you can find it in your heart to deprive the birds of them). Hawthorn (*Crataegus*) produces food for many birds, as does common elder (*Sambucus nigra*), which is a fast-growing, disorderly tree, best used in a boundary planting or in a very wild garden.

Other trees that provide bird meals (with edible seeds, or which attract many insects – food for the birds)

Alder, beech, birch, oak and willow.

Plants for shelter

Most evergreens and conifers (but avoid the fast-growing and un-neighbourly Leyland's cypress); dense hedges, shrubs and climbers.

Other plants

Almost anything that sets seed attracts birds in autumn and winter. These are guaranteed to bring them in: teasel, artichoke, sunflower, thistle, nettle, verbascum.

THE NECTAR SIPPERS

Butterflies and bees add a whimsical element to the garden, flitting delicately on floaty wings and buzzing around in striped or furry suits. Or so one might think when one is feeling all mawkish and intoxicated by nature.

Yet in the case of the bees, their airborne amblings play a critical part in the survival of many of this planet's species. Bees are the principal pollinators of plants: without their work there would be patchy (at best) yields of countless fruits, including all those mentioned above as foods for birds.

There would also be vastly diminished harvests of crops that human beings rely upon: apples, pears, cherries, currants, courgettes, pumpkins and many others. Likewise much non-fruit

Sea holly harmony: bumblebee, honeybee and wasp share the territory on the biennial *Eryngium giganteum*.

produce depends upon bees, because without their pollen-ferrying activities, the plants would not form the seed that is required for sowing the crops each year. Therefore without bees, onions, carrots, parsnips, celery and brassicas would also be in trouble. If there were no bees, a third of all human food crops would be in dire straits.

This grim situation is more than a hypothetical idea, for bees are in crisis, especially in America. There, a mysterious condition known as colony collapse disorder (CCD) is devastating populations of honeybees. Hive members simply fail to return to their colony, while the few that remain in the near-deserted hives are weakened by parasites and disease. Strangely, the abandoned wax and honey is not robbed by other bees or insect scavengers. Some bee experts attribute the disorder to widely used neonicotinoid pesticides, which they claim can cause disorientation, and a breakdown of immune systems. CCD is not confirmed in hives in Ireland and Britain, but varroa mite and cold, wet summers can cause disastrous losses. Bees on both sides of the Atlantic need all the help that we can give them.

NECTAR PUMPS FOR THE HONEYBEE

Gardeners can help honeybees by planting nectar- and pollen-rich plants, especially those that bloom at either end of the year, when not much else is in flower. Early bloomers include aubrieta, bluebell, crocus, euphorbia, hellebore, berberis, acacia, alder and willow (and dandelion too, if you have a wild area). For later in the year, consider aster, eupatorium, sedum, fuchsia, heather, ivy, mahonia and the aptly named beekeeper's tree (*Tetradrium daniellii*).

Honeybees have shorter tongues than bumblebees, and are unable to probe far enough inside some tubular blooms to reach the nectar. They prefer simple flowers, with open dish-shaped heads, or those where there is easy access to the nectaries. Almost all members of the rose family (although not multi-petalled garden roses) are favoured by honeybees: apple, cherry, pear, amelanchier, cotoneaster, pyracantha. Herbs belonging to the mint family (*Lamiaceae*) proffer lavish sups of nectar. Besides mint, these include catmint, lemon balm, rosemary, sage, thyme and many others.

The borage family (*Boraginaceae*) includes these honeybee plants: echium, forget-me-not, alkanet (*Anchusa*) and evergreen alkanet (*Pentaglottis*). The umbellifer family, which is known as *Apiaceae*, is also a hit with our honey-making insect friends (the family name comes from the Latin word *apis*, meaning bee). Among its members are fennel, dill, carrot and the sea

A honeybee coming in to land on an evergreen alkanet (*Pentaglottis sempervirens*), while a common carder bumblebee buzzes into a catmint (*Nepeta kubanica*).

hollies (*Eryngium*). Honeybees are also keen on members of the daisy clan, including the silvery-blue globe thistle (*Echinops*), and on cottage-garden plants with easy-to-reach nectar: allium, cornflower, hardy geraniums, *Knautia*, musk mallow, hollyhock and verbascum. It's worth mentioning here that many highly bred bedding and patio plants are poor providers of nectar and pollen. So while busy Lizzies, pansies and begonias may make great splashes of colour all summer, they are of little use to bees.

BUMBLEBEE BAR

Most bumblebees like tubular flowers. The foxglove is a favourite of two common species, *Bombus hortorum* and *B. pascuorum*, and it was designed by nature specifically with bumblebees in mind. The broad lip acts as a landing ledge, while its coating of hairs deters smaller insects from stopping in. When the bumblebee touches down, spots guide it inwards to the stamens and stigma, while the funnel-shaped flower neatly closes the bee's wings as it crawls towards the nectaries. This tight fit ensures that by the time the bee has finished its meal it is bountifully dusted with pollen. Bumblebees will forage for nectar in the plants recommended for honeybees (above). They are also fond of monkshood (*Aconitum carmichaelii*, *A. napellus* and cultivars), aquilegia, delphinium, lungwort (*Pulmonaria*), lupin, strawberry and raspberry.

A honeybee probing for nectar in a flower of evergreen alkanet; and a bumblebee on *Agastache*.

Unlike honeybees, bumblebees do not build up large stocks of honey in their homes. The fertile queen hibernates during the winter, and emerges in spring to start her new brood. However, with the current phenomenon of warmer winters, some bumblebees are out and about all year, and can be seen on clement days in milder regions. Winter-flowering plants are essential for their survival. In our garden, winter cherry (*Prunus* × *subhirtella* 'Autumnalis') and the sweet-scented shrub *Viburnum* × *bodnantense* 'Dawn' are in continual use on balmy winter days.

The bumblebee has a distinctive method of gathering pollen that is particularly sticky, or is otherwise reluctant to leave the anthers. The bee holds on to the flower and vibrates her flight muscles so that the pollen is shaken free. This process is called sonication, or buzz pollination, and makes a concentrated din, like a very small electric drill.

THE SOLITARY BEE

Of all the bee species in Britain and Ireland, the greatest number are solitary bees (about 200 and 80 respectively) – a category that includes the much-maligned leafcutter bees (*Megachile* spp.), so detested by rose growers. These lone insects live in holes, which may be in the ground, in dunes and cliffs, in soft masonry, in hollow or pithy plant stems or in bits of dead wood (as in old fence posts). Some species live in 'villages', where the tiny burrows are clustered together, while others share a common entrance, but each individual builds a separate nest within. All live only weeks as adults, and their larvae are left to fend for themselves – one reason why this group of bees has the 'solitary' label. When each egg is laid, however, minute portions of nectar and pollen are left with it in the nursery chamber. In the case of the leafcutter bees, the pieces of precisely scissored foliage are used to build these compartments – each of which is neatly closed with a leafy lid. I'm sure that if more rose growers knew the hard work that went into these creations, they would be happy to grant the accomplished craftswomen a few scraps of greenery, especially as the plant is never going to miss them.

A red admiral butterfly gorging on nectar supplied by the well-named butterfly bush (*Buddleja davidii*).

A small tortoiseshell butterfly hovering over a globe thistle (*Echinops*) flower.

BEAUTEOUS BUTTERFLIES

In our garden, the holly blue, an ethereal little thing with wings the colour of the Virgin Mary's mantle, is the first butterfly to appear, in March. Usually we have to wait a further two months before it is joined by others: the cabbage-devouring whites. It is the caterpillars of the latter that turn the leaves of brassicas to lace, as they chomp their way through your best broccoli and kale. Interspersing brassicas with other plants helps to confuse the female butterfly who is in search of a nourishing leaf on which to lay her eggs. And if you have only a few plants at any time (as we do), it is easy enough to inspect them every week or so, and to feed any caterpillars to a friendly robin or hen. Otherwise, it may be necessary to protect the crop with a net. The more flamboyant butterflies, such as the red admirals and small tortoiseshells, appear later in the summer, from July onwards.

All butterflies are cold blooded, and are governed by the temperature of the air. Their bodies must warm to 30–35°C (86–95°F) in order to fly, so sun and shelter are important. Supply them with heat-retaining slabs or rocks, where they can bask and warm up in preparation for flight; and mass together your nectar plants in the warmest part of the garden, where the accumulated smell and colour will attract them.

A small tortoiseshell butterfly attends to the flower of *Knautia arvensis*.

BUTTERFLY FARE

Aside from the caterpillars of the whites, there are no other butterfly larvae on these islands that are destructive to human crops. The adults have no mandibles, and dine exclusively on nectar, or, as I mentioned earlier – regarding the speckled wood and the holly blue – on the sugary, second-hand sap excreted by aphids. Butterflies do help – a little – to pollinate plants, and their caterpillars are a source of food for birds. But in the main they are just beautiful creatures to have around, and an indicator of a healthy level of biodiversity in a garden.

Butterflies will take nectar from many of the plants that I have already recommended for honeybees, especially asters, *Echinops,* eupatoriums, *Knautia* and large sedums. And if you plant the well-named butterfly bush, *Buddleja davidii,* it will be mobbed by nectar-seeking winged creatures. (You can keep this shrub from becoming too straggly by pruning its stems back to a third of their length each spring.) The lanky purple-topped *Verbena bonariensis* is another choice plant for butterflies; it will self-seed in mild gardens with not too heavy soil.

An important plant for the butterfly species that are likely to set up home in gardens is the nettle. Small tortoiseshells, peacocks and red admirals lay their eggs exclusively on this humble plant. Indeed, the Latin name for the small tortoiseshell is *Aglais urticae*, from *Urtica*, the nettle. Thistles are the food plant of the painted lady's offspring; holly and ivy feed the caterpillars of the holly blue; and grasses are the larval food of the speckled wood, the wall brown and a number of other less common species.

Peacock and small tortoiseshell butterflies supping nectar from eupatorium flower heads.

Let's not forget the less glitzy cousins of the butterflies, the moths. Many of these are abroad after dusk, searching for nectar in flowers that bloom in the evening, such as night-scented stock, tobacco plant and evening primrose. These night-flyers are liable to end up in the jaws of an aerobatic bat – another engaging wild creature that is part of the garden citizenry.

Bees and butterflies in decline

Since 1980, 3 of Ireland's 101 bee species have become extinct. The distribution of 42 other species has decreased by over 50 per cent, and that of 11 further species by over 30 per cent. A third of the Irish bee fauna is under threat of extinction. Britain is home to around 250 species of bee, although 2 of these are already extinct, and many others are endangered. Over half of British bumblebee species are listed as conservation priorities under the UK Biodiversity Action Plan.

Butterflies are in a similar predicament. In Britain, of the 59 resident species 5 have become extinct, and three-quarters are declining. On the other hand, 15 species are expanding their range, probably because of climate change. In Ireland, the mountain ringlet (*Erebia epiphron*) is extinct, and of the 33 remaining species of butterfly 6 others are under threat. These include two occasional visitors to Irish gardens: the wall brown (*Lasiommata megera*) and the small copper (*Lycaena phlaeas*).

HAPPY HABITATS FOR TINY CREATURES

Habitat loss and fragmentation, intensive agricultural practices, pesticide use and climate change are all factors that have led to declines in bee, butterfly and moth populations. They have also caused decreases in numbers of many other less glamorous invertebrates. Yet all are important contributors to the great interwoven eat-or-be-eaten mesh that is life in the garden.

Gardeners need not be concerned, however, with making a suitable habitat for each and every endangered species. A few simple steps will make the garden a congenial place for a variety of wildlife. For instance, as I've mentioned above, many of the plants that I've recommended for birds are also good for bees and for other invertebrates. A compost heap will attract all kinds of different species, as will a garden pond, a margin of long grass or a layer of leaf litter under the shrubs. A plant or habitat is rarely appealing to only one animal; instead it becomes a gathering place for a network of interdependent species.

Cutting down on pesticides is the obvious first step towards a more diverse garden. Most chemicals deal with an infestation only in the short term, and the pests (aphids, say, or white fly) reappear with a vengeance in days. Meanwhile, their predators, which have longer life cycles, take a greater time to recover. So once you start spraying, you are committed to regular outings with your poison bottle. In a balanced garden there are fewer scourges of pests. Crucial and early control can be achieved by vigilance, and by mechanical means of pest removal (in other words, stomping or squishing).

Gratifyingly, probably the single most effective thing you can do for wildlife in your garden is to stop being so tidy. I like that idea so much that I think I'll say it again: stop being so tidy! Imagine: we can free ourselves from the tyranny of tidiness, while doing a good turn for our fellow earthlings.

EDGY MATTERS

Let's consider the matter of the edges of a garden. Instead of keeping them all ship-shape and buttoned-down to the ground, why not let things become a bit looser? If you have grass running up to the boundaries of your property, stop mowing and trimming it along this outer edge – even a 45-centimetre (18-inch) strip will make a safe haven for invertebrates, and frogs, if they are in the area. Or if you have the space, think about creating a more natural perimeter of meadow, hedgerow, woodland, marsh – or whatever the conditions and the surrounding environment suggest.

Even a small wildish patch – no bigger than a double bed – can act as a refuge for many creatures: bumblebees will nest under tussocks of grass, at the bases of shrubs and in deserted mouse holes.

A pair of amorous ladybirds surrounded by the black aphids that will become their dinner.

Caterpillars will hang out in the long grass and nettles, and the latter plant will also be a roosting place for early aphids (which in turn become food for ladybirds). Beetles, centipedes and many other crawling things will trundle around under piles of leaves or brushwood. Spiders will weave their webs in undisturbed corners.

Many gardens today are enclosed by timber fence panels. These do a fine job of delineating a boundary, but hold minimal interest for wildlife, except for the odd earwig who might find sanctuary in the gaps between the boards. If there is enough room, a hedge is the very best perimeter for a garden: birds will nest and sleep in it, and a host of smaller wild things will take up residence. If the garden is too small for a hedge, climbers such as honeysuckle and clematis can be used to clothe a fence; both will need something to grab on to, such as sheep or chicken wire. If you have a sturdy wall or fence bordering your garden, consider ivy, which is self-clinging and needs no help to climb. It can damage a crumbling wall, so be careful where you let it grow. Still, it is a prime wildlife plant, providing protection from weather and predators, and supplying nectar, pollen and berries at otherwise frugal times of the year.

LEAVES AND OTHER GREEN STUFF
In the excessively tidy garden, autumn leaves are fussily whisked away the second they hit the ground. But there's no need to be in such a hurry to cart them away. Do remove them from lawns, paths and paving, and where they might smother plants. But you can let them lie on bare soil, or tuck them away out of sight under shrubs or at the backs of borders. Worms will eventually pull them underground, and in the meantime they will be colonized by many groups of invertebrates.

If you have lots of leaves, you can use them to make leafmould (see Chapter 9), or if you have just a moderate amount, you can add them to the compost. The compost heap itself sees concentrated activity on a scale that is unmatched anywhere else in the garden. The millions of individuals toiling, moiling, eating, living, dying and reproducing remind me of those frenzied paintings by Hieronymus Bosch or Pieter Brueghel the Elder – if you substitute garden critters for medieval Dutchmen.

THE LURE OF WATER
Water is as vital to wildlife as it is to humans. It can take the form of a pond or stream, or even a mini pool made from an old Belfast sink. Birds will drink from it and bathe in it, and many other creatures will visit it.

A pond, such as this, edged with plants (here, primulas and arum lilies) is a magnet for wildlife.

A felled paulownia tree has a new lease of life as a wildlife-friendly log sculpture, with holes drilled for invertebrates; a wildlife 'hotel' made from old shipping pallets.

Honeybees, for example, who take water back to their hive to cool it: they fan the liquid until it evaporates and lowers the temperature. Small mammals and foxes also use garden ponds as watering holes. Frogs (and newts, if you are lucky) will set up home in a hospitable body of water. Make sure that at least one side is graduated or stepped so that there is safe access, and so that birds can perch in the shallows and flick water over themselves.

SPECIALIZED ACCOMMODATION

You can also make more specific habitats for particular groups of mini beasts. Log piles metamorphose into a miniature ecosystem after a few months, as they are attacked by fungi and other micro-organisms. Stack the wood horizontally, or stand the logs on end, like a gathering of ancient columns (bury their bases to prevent toppling, if necessary). In time they will attract woodlice, ground beetles, stag beetles, millipedes, centipedes, spiders, slugs, snails and larger creatures such as frogs, toads and hedgehogs.

You can construct a dormitory for solitary bees by taking a block of wood, or a log, and drilling it with holes, 6–10 millimetres wide and 15 centimetres deep. Position it about 1.5 metres (5 feet) above the ground, facing south, so that the openings are horizontal. Or for more spontaneous housing, you can quickly tie together short lengths of hollow stems. Other invertebrates besides solitary bees may move in, and you may find you have a more diverse mix of residents.

Bat boxes give these tiny flying mammals somewhere to roost (the Bat Conservation Trust website has links to bat box plans: see Resources, page 204). Modern homes, which are well sealed and lacking in gaps and crevices, offer few opportunities for bats to find a daytime resting place. Boxes, preferably more than one, should be placed in sheltered areas, facing in different directions so that each has a different temperature. This way, the bats can choose one to suit their needs on a particular day.

SOME OTHER GOODIES

I've already mentioned many of the animals in our gardens that can be considered our allies: the bees, butterflies and moths that act as pollinators, and the birds, bats, frogs, ladybirds, spiders, centipedes and ground beetles that dine on the plant-eaters. There are other carnivores as well that are keen on aphids: hoverfly and lacewing larvae are predators, as are several tiny parasitic wasps. These deposit single eggs in the bodies of young aphids, and the resulting grubs eat their hosts from the inside out. (I never said nature was pretty.) Larger wasps – the ones that become such a nuisance in late summer – are also aphid-eaters, so can be cautiously welcomed as associates.

Worms, of course, are also our firm friends, as they heroically till the soil, aerate it and lace it through with organic matter – as I mentioned earlier (see page 28).

THE BADDIES: NOT SO BAD AFTER ALL?

By now, I hope you're beginning to notice that the baddies are not *all* bad *all* the time. I mean, if you are a greenfinch in the cold, empty-larder days of early spring, a family gathering of aphids on the swelling buds of a rose is a very good thing indeed. And if you're a blackbird, starling or jackdaw, a lawn that is lousy with leatherjackets, the globby larvae of craneflies, is a grand place for a feed. Likewise, a hungry thrush will be more than happy to see a fat snail motoring slowly across the pavement. (Still, in deference to mollusc-embattled gardeners in Ireland and the damper parts of Britain, I will offer more advice on slugs and snails below.)

As I said earlier, if you create the conditions that welcome a great range of creatures to your garden, they more likely to maintain order among themselves. This isn't to say that I sit around watching slugs wreaking havoc among my lettuces and blackfly sucking the lifeblood from my beans. No, I bump off small plant-eating brutes all the time, by the quickest means possible (hand-to-hand combat, a scrunching boot or a blast of the hose). Vigilance, followed by a swift dispatch, are the methods I use most frequently.

I believe in outwitting pests whenever possible: by excluding them with a physical barrier, by trapping them, by making the conditions uncongenial to them and by timing planting or other operations to avoid their peak periods of activity. I also believe in interplanting a pest's target plant species with others that have no interest for them or that repel them (you'll find more on this in Chapter 9). I rarely use biological controls, such as the nematodes or predators that come in a packet (available from certain garden centres), but they can be effective if you have a serious problem. I'm not put out by a certain amount of pest damage: I don't aim for a garden where every plant has the unblemished appearance of a Hollywood hottie. I'm more interested in a garden that 'lives', with plants and animals all getting on with their intersecting businesses.

THINGS THAT SLITHER IN THE NIGHT: SLUGS AND SNAILS

At some point in every beginner gardener's career, plants do an overnight vanishing act. At lunchtime on Wednesday there is a hopeful row of bright-green lettuce seedlings, promising a steady supply of cool, fresh salads in the weeks ahead. But before breakfast on Thursday – incomprehensibly – they have disappeared without a trace.

Most likely, it is slugs or snails (or both) that have passed over the lettuces in the dark hours, rasping them into their maws with their serrated radulae (or mouth parts). It's hard not to take this sort of wholesale destruction personally, and so war is immediately declared against the blobby hordes of gastropods.

The first rule of war, though, is to know your enemy. Intelligence must be gathered, facts separated from fiction and appropriate strategies devised. Therefore let us first consider the snail, and then the slug. (Molluscs are the pests about which the Royal Horticultural Society advisory service gets the most queries, making them Number One Bad Guys.)

The snail that causes the most damage is the garden snail (*Helix aspera*), purposefully sliding along with its familiar brown house on its back. The white-lipped banded snail (*Cepaea hortensis*) with its jazzy stripes and the tiny dull-brown strawberry snail (*Trichia striolata*) are less voracious, but still worth keeping an eye on. Actually, I'm quite fond of snails (when I'm feeling especially in tune with the world), and admire their perfectly formed shells and their daintily questing tentacles, the lower pair, which act as feelers, dabbing the ground in front, and the upper ones swaying about like a brace of flexuous periscopes.

I even admire slugs, especially the spectacular black slug (*Arion ater*), a walrus of a creature which – despite the 'black' in its moniker – may also be orange, brown or khaki. When at rest it is a rotundly Rubenesque bulge-being, yet when gliding along at full stretch it is transformed into a slick and sinuous athlete, 10 centimetres (4 inches) or more long.

Alas, poor *Arion ater*, it is the first mollusc that draws fire from the gardener, just because it is so big, and so gloopy. But in fact, it is one of the least destructive of slugs. Although it is partial to the odd seedling and lettuce leaf, its diet is more likely to consist of rotting matter, so its good deeds outweigh its occasional lapses. Far more destructive are the garden slug (*Arion hortensis*), with its slim, black-grey body and orange undercarriage; and the revoltingly mucilaginous grey field slug (*Deroceras reticulatum*). The keeled slug (*Tandonia* and *Milax* spp.), which has a ridge along its back (hence the name), and which may be grey, brown or black, is also a hostile force in the garden. Much of its work is carried on underground, where it mashes into potatoes and other root crops.

All slugs and snails are hermaphrodite (having both sets of reproductive tackle), which means that they are in the happy situation whereby each and every member of their species that they meet is a potential sexual partner. After mating, which can take some hours, both partners go off and lay eggs, in crevices in the soil and in other damp, dark places (including the potting medium in plant containers). Hundreds of eggs – like tiny pearls, or minuscule, gelatinous balloons – may be laid in a season. They must remain moist in order to hatch, as dry air or hot sunshine means certain death to the embryos inside.

Adult slugs and snails can't cope with dry conditions either: their muscular mass must

The common snail (*Helix aspera*) can do a lot of damage, while the huge and blobby black slug (*Arion ater*) is often unfairly blamed for other molluscs' crimes.

remain clammy and supple in order to glide over surfaces. (The name gastropod, which means 'stomach foot', is vividly apt.) Garden gastropods, therefore, are most active when there is more humidity: after dusk; on dull, overcast days; and after rainfall, especially if it follows a dry spell. Excessive rain and air temperatures below 5°C (41°F) also drive them into their sheltered hiding places, or underground. Our changing climate, however, means that we're more likely to find a hungry mollusc out foraging on a balmy winter's day.

STRATEGIES

Over the years, I've discovered that the best way to deal with the gastropod problem is to adopt a multi-pronged approach: some defensiveness, some common sense, some ingenuity and a bit of cold-blooded slaughter. I also recommend some stoicism. Slugs and snails are out there in the garden round the clock, doing what they do, whereas the gardener can spend only so much time campaigning against them. If you lose sight of this, the garden takes on all the tensions and traumas of a battleground. The most foolproof plan, obviously, is to grow only plants that are slug and snail resistant (see list below), but that would rule out many plants, including some leafy vegetables – which are among the most rewarding things to raise.

- **Cultivate cleverly**: When sowing seeds, start them in seed trays or modules, where possible. Plant them in the garden at the plantlet stage, when they are less vulnerable than tender seedlings (and reserve some extras to fill the gaps left after the inevitable losses). When planting, water the bottom of the hole or trench, insert your plantlet and water again *in the* *hole,* if necessary. Then pull dry soil back over the root ball. Don't water again for a few days, as a wet soil surface around plants offers the ideal foothold for a marauding mollusc. If you have to water vulnerable plants, do it in the morning, rather than the evening. Interplant tempting species, such as lettuce and hosta, with other, non-desirable plants. Don't edge your vegetable beds with grass, as the soft and pleasant texture offers the equivalent of an extensive green welcome mat.

- **Build barriers**: Guard susceptible plants by encircling them with tall collars made from plastic drinks bottles. Or surround them with grit, wood ash, dried and crushed egg shells or dried grass clippings. These materials work to varying degrees in different gardens, and the resulting barriers need to be continually maintained. Leaves or other matter spanning them can act as bridges. Remember that wood ash is alkaline, and may change the pH of the soil. Snails and slugs don't like to pass over copper. You can buy copper tape to stick around pots: it is expensive, but may be worth considering for containers of choice plants such as hostas. Likewise, you can gird pots with a band of petroleum jelly, but this can get messy.

- **Go hunting**: Seek out the enemy on mild, damp evenings, and during your daily gardening activities keep an eye out for their cool and damp daytime refuges: in the crevices in walls, under slabs and among piles of pots. Favourite retreats also include dense evergreen plants, such as box hedging and clumps of agapanthus. Dispose of the culprits quickly and cleanly. I snip them in two with scissors (the squeamishness abates after a few sessions) or slice them speedily with a sharp trowel. I don't know if slugs and snails feel pain, but I figure that an instant end is 'kinder' than throwing them into a bucket of salty water (as some gardeners do) or offering some other prolonged death. Anyway, what do you do with a bucket of environmentally damaging salty slug soup?

- **Go trapping**: Create slug-friendly sanctuaries under slates, grapefruit skins or melon rinds. Place them in the corners of vegetable beds, and clear out the sheltering molluscs every day.

- **Practise birth control**: Destroy the eggs before they hatch. Look for them in clusters near the soil surface and in pots of moist compost. It's not unusual to catch a snail in the act of laying eggs.

- **Offer drinks**: Gastropods can't resist a sup of beer, and they don't know when to stop. Sink a container (such as a yoghurt carton) into the soil and fill with beer. Leave a lip of a centimetre above the soil surface, so that ground beetles don't fall in. Remove the corpses daily, and change the beer when it gets disgusting (after about three days). This is practicable only in small areas, but is useful in greenhouses and other enclosures. Fruit juice and milk are also supposed to do the trick, but I can't vouch for them.

- **Call in the nematodes**: Eelworms that parasitize slugs and some small snails are available from a few garden shops and by mail order. As with beer, they are not a cheap solution, but are invaluable for clearing a greenhouse.

- **Lay poison**: Traditional molluscicide pellets contain either methiocarb or metaldehyde. Both can be harmful to non-target species, and have no place in a wildlife-friendly garden, especially as there is now an alternative, based on iron phosphate. These pellets are non-toxic to other garden inhabitants including soil creatures, birds and pets; and they break down harmlessly in the soil. Slugs and snails that eat them increase mucus production, stop feeding and die within days. (None of which is a pretty thought, but if we're using poisons, we should know what they do.) Usually the dying creatures go away to expire, so there are no bodies around – unlike with conventional pellets.

PLANTS RESISTANT TO SLUGS AND SNAILS

In the ornamental garden, there are a few plants that are guaranteed to be destroyed by our gastropod friends, so first of all, I'd like to recommend that if you want an easy life, avoid hostas, delphiniums, lupins, dahlias, and – if you're a posh gardener – the Chatham island forget-me-not (*Myosotidium hortensia*). There are hundreds of other plants that are slug and snail proof. Here are a few of the more common ones.

Perennials that are resistant to slugs and snails include: bear's breeches (*Acanthus spinosus*), lady's mantle (*Alchemilla mollis*), Japanese anemones, columbine (*Aquilegia*), sea pink (*Armeria*), arum, astilbe, astrantia, bergenia, dicentra, hardy geraniums, globe thistle (*Echinops*), sea holly (*Eryngium*), euphorbia, geum, *Knautia macedonica*, toad flax (*Linaria*), lysimachia, plume poppy (*Macleaya*), oriental poppy (*Papaver*), peony, penstemon, bistort (*Persicaria*), Solomon's seal (*Polygonatum*), sedum, sisyrinchium, verbascum, *Verbena bonariensis*, veronica, periwinkle (*Vinca*), most ferns, most ornamental grasses.

Annuals and biennials include: pot or English marigold (*Calendula*), cornflower (*Centaurea cyanus*), foxglove (*Digitalis*), teasel (*Dipsacus*), echium, poached-egg plant (*Limnanthes*), forget-me-not (*Myosotis*), love-in-a-mist (*Nigella*), annual poppies (*Papaver*), nasturtium (*Tropaeolum majus*).

One of the lesser periwinkles (*Vinca minor* 'Argenteovariegata'): slugs and snails don't bother it or its relatives.

Our old rooster, Bosie, makes some loud comments in the compost area.

In the edible (edible for humans, that is) garden, most herbs are mollusc proof (although not basil). Members of the legume, marrow and brassica families need protection when infants, but are able to fend off the attentions of slugs and snails when more mature. Lettuce is very prone to damage, but red-leaved varieties are more resistant; the same is true for oriental leaves such as pak choi. The following potatoes are more resistant to attack from underground slugs than most: 'Ambo', 'Cara', 'Charlotte', 'Desiree', 'Kestrel', 'Orla', 'Pentland Dell', 'Romano', 'Sante', 'Ulster Chieftain' and 'Valor'.

A WORD ABOUT CHICKENS

After nearly ten years of keeping hens in our sixth-of-an-acre town garden, I am thinking about de-henning – as soon as our magnificent Bosie crows his way into the next world. Females can be given away, as people are happy to accept an egg-layer. But I would not try to re-home our elderly and esteemed rooster: we've been through too much together. Part of what we're still going through, incidentally, is that every single night, either my husband or I has to collect him from the hen house (or, on clement nights, from the branches of the Persian ironwood) and put him into a soundproof compartment in the garage. With a couple of dozen households within crowing distance, we try to keep early mornings as peaceful as possible.

Our hens have always free-ranged. We don't have enough room for a decent-sized run, and I would not like to confine them to a tiny space. Therefore, every newly planted item must be protected with a hand-built cage of bamboo stems, birch twigs or whatever is at hand: freshly turned earth is an invitation to scratch for creepy-crawlies and worms. And our vegetable beds, with their juicy lettuces and other interesting greens, must be netted to prevent swift beaks reducing the leaves to their central ribs.

The fox was a constant worry, until we installed an electrified wire around the top of our garden wall. So with the plants caged in, and the fox wired out, our hens have had quite a bit of influence on our garden structure.

If you have a rooster and hens, you soon have chicks, which are pretty and cute, until they grow up into more cocks and hens – more than a town garden can support. So homes must be sought, unless you are prepared to eat the excess fowl.

As with childbirth, there are unspoken things about keeping chickens. It's not natural for a bird to lay hundreds of eggs a year. They get worn out and less productive. That's why laying hens are culled after a period of time in poultry farms. But with pet chickens, no one is going to terminate Henny Penny's life just because she is a non-paying investment. No, we keep her on into glorious old-ladyhood, and we're grateful when she manages to squeeze out an egg or two from her tired old anatomy. But meanwhile, her egg-laying apparatus is deteriorating, and that, let me assure you, can be distressing to behold. A hen with a chronically prolapsed oviduct is a piteous thing. Someone has to put her out of her misery. I could go on in this vein indefinitely, but don't want to seem too much of a killjoy. I just want to urge you, before you get hens, to think of those hens getting old and work out how to deal with their demise in a humane manner.

The other side of this is that backyard hens produce the tastiest, freshest eggs in the world, their manure is dynamite for the compost heap and they clean up a fair number of garden pests – in between the unlawful sabotaging of seedlings and grazing of greens. Also, hens are endlessly entertaining and educational. Their behaviour to each other is not far off that of humans – but without the inhibitions. Our fowl friends do to each other the things that humans are restrained from doing by politeness or the law. If you're a chicken and you don't like someone, you simply clobber them on the back of the head with your beak. Or, if another hen finds a big worm that looks good to you, there is nothing to stop you from making a lunge for it.

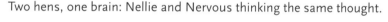

Two hens, one brain: Nellie and Nervous thinking the same thought.

FOOD

'I came to love my rows, my beans, though so many more than I wanted. They attached me to the earth, and so I got strength like Antaeus.'
Henry David Thoreau, *Walden*

In her last decade, my mother lived for her vegetable garden. She was ill with cancer, but there was sense, some order and much vitality in her garden. It saved her life many times. This was a part of nature that she could control and make fruitful, while another part, over which she was powerless, was fatally draining her life force.

This may sound sad, but – aside from the fact that she was dying – my mother was happier than she had been for years. In her letters to her children (we had all left home, which at that point was in Minnesota), she would comment dutifully on family matters and other items, and then move straight on to the subject that she really cared about: the garden.

Her garden was not a green and pastoral place of pretty, herb-edged beds. It was a war zone. This was rural Minnesota, where a resistance movement of crop-destroying varmints (a word she read in *Organic Gardening* magazine and liked to repeat) was ever present. On thin airmail paper, her faint and grey typed words (she was not one to change the typewriter ribbon readily) told tales of pocket gophers, raccoons, squirrels, mice, voles, rabbits, chipmunks and deer. They circled the perimeter of her vegetable patch, searching for a torn piece of netting, a dip in the barricade or a tunnel made by a previous saboteur. Once in, they mowed down seedlings, chewed through the bulges on swelling pea pods, scattered raspberries – both ripe and not – on the ground and mangled hard-won melons the night before harvest. Invertebrate pests attacked also, invading by air and land; constant battles were waged with cutworms, cabbage loopers and other offenders.

If it wasn't some kind of critter that was out to get her crops, it was the weather: temperatures zinged from freezing to blistering overnight, and meteorological cataclysms threatened often: tornadoes, high winds, torrential rain and June hailstones – 'golf-ball size, but flat, not ball shape, about three-quarter inch thick . . . like those French paper weights'.

To tell the truth, she enjoyed the fight, and enjoyed the creative surge she got while inventing or amending plant supports, barriers and traps. Found or discarded items were pressed into

A healthy crop of chilli peppers in our conservatory: the fruits are pickled or dried, and last all year.

My mother, Betty Wahl Powers, in her Minnesota vegetable patch in the 1980s.

service – indeed, into several serial services – to make or modify the devices essential to the pioneering life in the 1970s and '80s organic vegetable lot. 'I bought a live trap', she wrote, to save the strawberries that were being 'chipmunked out of existence'. But the trap, a 'faulty design', as she noted with just a hint of superiority, was a failure until it was remedied 'with auxiliary structures of coffee cans and cottage cheese cartons and egg boxes and . . . weights of brick and stone'. (The improved version soon caught not a chipmunk but a vole – which, like its fellow villains, was biked off the property and released by the lake.) Her raw materials for her engineering projects included tobacco tins, decommissioned ice hockey sticks, a dog run that someone had thrown out and plenty of old bits of lumber and string (the latter unravelled from an abandoned macramé hammock that my father had foraged for her).

What she enjoyed most, though, was the produce that her fiercely contested patch – assiduously mulched with leaves, grass clippings and compost – gave her during the short but eventful Minnesota summer. Her autumn letters are content and triumphant, filled with satisfied inventories of fruits and vegetables harvested, preserved, pickled, frozen and dried. As the Midwestern winter hid her dormant garden under drifts of snow, the bounty from the soil fattened her larder and basement. And after her death, my father – no food-grower, although he had helped her willingly – dined for more years than was safe on her stockpiled provisions.

I never want my garden to look like my mother's, because it was a crazy, gently exhibitionist place that proudly carried notions of self-sufficiency to the extreme. However, in retrospect, I admire her ability to re-use things creatively and fearlessly, at a time when it was not fashionable to do so.

And in her way, she was gardening with nature, or at least the parts of it that weren't out to wreak havoc with her crops. She welcomed the garter snakes and toads, and approved of their diets, which consisted mainly of the creatures that were dining at her expense. She saw the sense of serving and preserving the fruits and vegetables that grew outside her door, rather than eating from the shelves of the supermarket, where the food had landed from who knew where. Her produce was free from pesticides and fertilizers, and was fresher than anything else available to her. Working the land gave her a positive charge when her spirit was depleted with uncertainty and distress. I'm mentioning my mother here, not just because I want to remember her, but because her gardening principles are relevant today, a time when we realize the importance of living lightly on, and in tune with, the Earth.

GETTING IT RIGHT: HARD-LEARNED ADVICE

I'm a poor gardener compared to my mother, and my challenges are tiny in this relatively tame climate and largely pest-free country (sure, we have slugs and snails, but their damage is nothing compared to the diggings of a single pocket gopher or the appetite of a family of squirrels). Still, I have learned a few things in my several decades of food growing.

One of those things has as much to do with human nature as with the business of gardening. You can cut out a lot of unhappiness if you grow only the food that you and the people you live with like to eat. With this in mind, let's talk about the cabbage family (brassicas). There is no doubt that the mature cabbage is a beautiful thing: it has good colour, and it cuts a heroic and monumental figure in the garden. But for certain people the brassica conjures up memories of repugnant school dinners in steamy-windowed dining halls: they'd rather run four laps around the soccer pitch than let a forkful of the green stuff pass their lips. If you are one of these individuals, it's unlikely you'll enjoy your sprouts, cabbage or kale any better just because you grew them. So either don't plant them, or try just one or two and see how you get on.

It may not be brassicas that you or your family find objectionable; it could be parsnips, or carrots, or coriander. Whatever it is, avoid it or go easy on it at first. There is nothing so demoralizing for a gardener as growing stuff that no one will eat. I know this advice sounds

Well-ordered vegetable beds in the Bay Garden, Co. Wexford.

blindingly obvious, but apparently it's not. A friend with an allotment tells me that all around her people grow Brussels sprouts, but no one eats them – and in springtime there is a sulphurous smell of forlorn and rotting sprout on the air.

One of the reasons that people grow food they dislike is that they get free seeds – often included with a gardening magazine – and they can't bear to 'waste' them. (I've fallen into this trap myself.) But when you think about it, isn't it a much greater waste to go to all the trouble of growing the seeds, when you may not even like what they turn into? Which brings me to another piece of counsel: when you are sowing seed, don't sow the whole packet. Some crop varieties (most lettuces, for instance) may have hundreds of seeds per packet. It's unlikely that you'll be wanting 200 mature lettuces in the space of one week. For crops such as this, which tend to peak over a short period, sow small amounts every few weeks.

You can't store lettuce, but most other products of the kitchen garden can be conserved in some way, by bottling, freezing, pickling or drying. It can be tiresome to have to do a preserving or freezing session at the end of a day in the garden, but in the following months you'll be happy you took the time. A full freezer, incidentally, uses less energy than a half-empty one.

When choosing what vegetables to grow, go for disease- and pest-resistant varieties. Before you decide which to buy, read the catalogues, or the information on the packets. Remember, though, that 'resistant' doesn't mean that the plants are impervious to the affliction in question:

A healthy crop of leeks looking quite decorative, with their blue-grey leaves.

it means that they have some degree of immunity. They may still suffer, but not as badly as a more vulnerable variety. And choose vegetables to suit your soil and conditions. Breeders have done their best to improve modern varieties, and to make them more adaptable to a wider range of conditions, but particular vegetables still prefer particular kinds of soil and climate. For example, while you may be able to grow melons outdoors in Ireland and the UK, you're unlikely to get a bountiful yield. If you're growing for novelty and show-off value, that's grand, but don't be planning on feeding a multitude.

SMALL GARDEN: NO ROOM FOR FOOD?

As I mentioned earlier, there is nothing to stop you including good-looking edibles among your other plants. Runner beans, Swiss chard with coloured stems and 'Bull's Blood' beetroot are all pretty enough to hold their own in any garden. Leeks are also fine-looking things, with their staunch, blue-hued leaves ('Bleu de Solaise' and 'St Victor' are among the bluest), and some kales are sculptural and well coloured ('Redbor' and the Tuscan 'Cavalo Nero'). Indeed, I think that all vegetables are handsome, especially if they are grown with an eye for design (Joy Larkcom's *Creative Vegetable Gardening* is the best book I know on this subject).

In recent years there has been much breeding of dwarf vegetables. Endearingly neat as they are, there is not much point in growing most of them in beds, as their yield is so small. A full-sized plant may occupy the same ground space as a dwarf one, but is taller and has more

The strangely crinkled Tuscan kale 'Cavalo Nero' in garden writer Joy Larkcom's patch; salad leaves grown as a cut-and-come-again crop.

Most herbs – such as the oregano, mint and basil shown here – are happy in pots. Keep them near the kitchen so you don't have far to travel when cooking.

fruits (which is technically what lots of vegetables are). However, if you are looking for petite plants to grow in containers, the dwarf kinds are ideal. Thanks to these introductions, you can cultivate aubergines, French and runner beans, peas and other edibles on a balcony or on a small patio.

Baby salad leaves, including lettuce, rocket, oriental leaves, chard and spinach, can also be grown in containers. You can harvest by picking the leaves individually, or by shearing them all off with scissors, when they are a few centimetres tall. This latter method is known as cut-and-come-again; the plants yield two to four such harvests before they tire.

Most herbs, of course, can also be grown in pots. The tall umbelliferous ones, such as fennel and dill, grow too lanky for all except very large pots, but they make stately garden plants in their own right. They attract hoverflies and wasps, both of which help to keep aphid numbers down.

If you do have room for a vegetable bed, but only a little one, concentrate on food that is difficult to buy in the shops. You might like to try baby vegetables (not to be confused with the dwarf ones above). These are harvested when they are just succulent mouthfuls: bijou beetroot, carrots, turnips, swedes. They are in and out of the ground quickly, and you can put different crops in their place the minute the soil is free – giving you an assortment of food from a small patch of soil. If I could grow only one kind of crop, it would be salad leaves – but more on that later.

WHAT VEGETABLES LIKE

We demand a lot from our edible plants. Unlike their less useful, but more ornamental fellows, they are expected to produce great volumes of nutritious material in a relatively short time. They need a lot of help to do this. They must have good soil: the best stuff in the garden. And that soil must be regularly topped up with fertility-boosting organic matter to replenish the nutrients that have been taken out by the crops. If you have enough garden compost, add two wheelbarrow loads (about 180 litres) per 10 square metres (108 square feet) of ground annually. Or, if you want a smaller unit of measurement, use a black plastic builders' bucket: you need about a bucket and a quarter per square metre (11 square feet). If you can get farmyard manure, use about half this amount, but make sure that the material is well rotted first. It should be stacked under a tarpaulin or other cover for at least six months (a year is preferable). These quantities are only a rough guide. Fertile soils will need less, and poorer ones more. Some crops are hungrier than others: runner beans and cabbages, for example, are quite greedy, while carrots and lettuce fare better on a leaner diet.

Your kitchen crops will need full sun, so be prepared to give them a choice spot in the garden. Beware of frost pockets: dips in the landscape that gather and hold frost. Shelter is also essential, as the adverse effects of wind are several. It dries out plant tissues and soil, destabilizes roots and makes photosynthesis more difficult. Chloroplasts – the parts of the plant that use sunlight to manufacture carbohydrates – are like the organism's solar panels, and are mostly located near the upper leaf surface. When the wind whooshes a plant around, it can turn the solar panels away from the sun, so there is less photosynthesis and less growth. Where there is room, a hedge offers the best shelter, as it diffuses the breeze, while also acting as a habitat for wildlife. You could have an edible hedge with nuts and fruits, or a living willow fence (a fedge). In very exposed areas, it's a good idea to erect a screen of polyethylene windbreak netting before planting a hedge, to give it a chance to establish itself. You could also could grow a temporary shelter belt of Jerusalem artichokes, which produce edible tubers, delicious in soup. These sunflower relatives come with two little warnings, though. When you are tired of them, be sure to remove every scrap of root and tuber from the soil, as they can be persistent. And they are not a vegetable for sociable eating, as they provoke heroic amounts of flatulence. If you still want to try them, the cultivar 'Fuseau' is less knobbly than some and is easier to clean for cooking.

Speaking of wind – back to the meteorological kind – a certain amount of air movement in the vegetable plot is a good thing. A stagnant atmosphere favours fungal diseases, so if there is a gentle zephyr playing around your crops, you have the perfect growing environment.

Vegetables need moisture. In the wetter parts of these islands, rain will do most of the watering for you. But if you live in a drier area and have free-draining soil, you will need to water occasionally. Mulch when the soil is wet, to preserve the moisture. Crucial periods for watering include the times when you are putting in plants and when flowers and fruits are appearing.

Vegetables are popular with rabbits. If bunnies are in the area, they will be eager to browse on your greens, beans and everything else. A rabbit-proof fence is the only thing that will deter them: it should be about 1 metre (39 inches) high, with the lowest 30 centimetres (12 inches) buried in the soil and angled outwards to prevent burrowing close to the barrier.

PUTTING YOUR CROPS TO BED

I'm a firm believer in using a system of individual beds for growing food. This arrangement makes sense in so many ways, not least because it confers instant tidiness on the vegetable plot. If your beds are weedy or empty, they still have a semblance of neatness. Beds, especially raised beds, put manners on a plot: they bring it into line, make it stand up straight and take its hands out of its pockets. The eye sees the orderly framework of rectangles before it alights on their contents. If you make the beds 90–120 centimetres (3–4 feet) wide, you can reach into the middle from either side. At this width, you never need to walk on them and the soil doesn't get compacted. Weeding and planting are so much easier when the soil consistency is more open and springy, and roots find it easier to travel. Beds are perfect for a no-dig or once-dig system: the latter is where you give the soil an initial dig to remove persistent weeds and incorporate organic material.

You can plant more densely in a narrow bed, because you don't need space to walk between the rows of vegetables. And because you use soil amendments (compost, manure, etc.) only in the actual growing area, they don't get wasted and trodden underfoot between rows, as they do in a non-bed system.

Beds can be either on the flat or raised. Soil warms up more quickly in raised beds, and excess moisture drains away more easily. This latter feature is very desirable in areas of high rainfall. Simple elevated beds can be made just by mounding up the soil a few centimetres – which does, it must be said, look a little like a freshly filled-in grave at first. But the cemetery look disappears as soon as the soil sprouts a few plants. Or you can edge the beds with brick, stone, blocks, timber, logs or various other materials. I've seen wine bottles, roofing tiles and plastic boards used to hold soil in place. In the past, our own raised beds have been edged with slates (snails love the interstices), salvaged pavers and scaffolding planks rescued from a skip.

Raised beds may be any length you want: just be aware that the weight of the soil will bow out the sides if you use long stretches of too-light timber. Remember also that you have to walk around the bed to get to the other side, so be prepared for a hike if you make them particularly long. As regards height: 60–70 centimetres (24–28 inches) is the right elevation for people who use wheelchairs or are not able to bend easily. A more usual height, however, is around 15–38 centimetres (6–15 inches).

Setting up a garden with raised beds may be more expensive than just growing things on the flat, but it is worth it, in my view. Besides the advantages mentioned above, it makes the rotating of crops easy to manage.

Raised beds, such as these at Glebe Gardens, Co. Cork, put manners on a plot, and help make rotation easier to organize.

ROTATION, ROTATION, ROTATION

Crop rotation was something I first heard about in geography class. Our teacher, who was more interested in cultivating her fingernails than her students, failed to explain the reasoning behind this agricultural juggling, so for years the words 'crop rotation' made me feel a little distracted. Now, however, I have a healthy respect for this method of managing soil and plants.

If you grow the same kinds of crops year after year in the same ground, pests and diseases that are specific to those plant groups build up in the soil. At the same time, certain nutrients become depleted. The soil, in other words, can become sick and tired. When you change the crops regularly, the ground has a chance to recover.

The easiest plan to follow is a three-year one, which means that with three beds, or three distinct areas in your vegetable-growing arrangement, you can grow all crops every year. Here's how it goes in year one: in the first bed, you grow only roots, including beetroot, carrot, parsnip and potato (but not turnips or swedes, which are brassicas); in the second bed you grow brassicas (all those cabbagey things, including the aforementioned turnips and swedes); and in the third, you grow everything else: courgette, lettuce, onion family, spinach and legumes (peas and beans). In subsequent years, you just move the crops one bed over: roots should be followed by brassicas, brassicas are followed by 'everything else', and 'everything else' is followed by roots. It's a simple process, possibly easier to explain in a diagram than in words.

For more serious growers, there are four- and five-year rotation plans based on different plant groups (and there are even longer schemes for fanatics). The model gardener keeps track of the crops in a notebook, or on big labels stuck in the beds. Although I always plan to be, I'm not that organized, and I rely on my memory – which is, at best, limited to a two-year time span. As a consequence, my own rotation methods are somewhat scatty: potatoes, brassicas and beans are moved around every year – the first two because they are disease prone, and the last because it's easy to remember where the towering wigwams of beans stood the previous season. Other vegetables are squeezed in wherever there is space. So far, my food crops have been healthy enough.

If your vegetables are hit with some horrible affliction, such as onion white rot (known also as 'mouldy nose', which makes it seem more personable) or brassica clubroot, don't grow susceptible crops in the same bed for as many years as possible. Both of the above disorders can persist in the soil for a very long time: eight to ten years in the case of white rot, and up to two decades for clubroot.

The 'three sisters', corn, beans and squash, growing at Dunmore Country School, in Co. Laois (the beans are still young and not too prominent).

A jumble of runner beans, lettuces and collard greens in my small vegetable patch.

Some timely advice: don't accept young plants of onions or brassicas unless you know that they come from a disease-free garden. Fungal spores are invisible, and it takes just one contaminated plant to infect your soil.

GOOD COMPANIONS

The 'three sisters', a traditional Native American planting system, is an ancient example of companion planting – where crops are grown together in a mutually beneficial way. The sisters in question are corn (maize), beans and squash. The corn offers a climbing frame for the beans and shade for the squash; the beans enrich the soil by fixing nitrogen in the nodules on their roots, while their twining stems act as guy ropes to stabilize the corn; and the huge leaves of the rambling squash vines serve as a living mulch over the soil, suppressing weeds and reducing evaporation.

Growing different crops together is known as intercropping. It has numerous benefits to the vegetable gardener. As the 'three sisters' admirably demonstrates, it keeps the soil covered and active; it makes it possible to grow a quantity of crops in a small space; it offers shade, shelter and support for vulnerable plants.

Another intercropping option is to grow a fast-maturing crop with a more leisurely one. In our garden, I often plant rocket and lettuce under our bean wigwams. They occupy ground that would be either empty or weedy, and they benefit from the increased moisture and the light shade. By the time the beans have run up the supports and enclosed the interior space in a green tent, we've had a good harvest of salad leaves. Radish, spring onions, oriental leaves and salad leaves are other quick crops that you can slide in between slower-growing ones.

Sociable planting may also confuse or repel pests. Crop-destroying insects are more likely to converge on an area clearly advertising a single kind of vegetable. Mixing unrelated species together cuts down on damage. Research has shown that cabbages interplanted with beans or clover suffer less damage from cabbage aphid and cabbage root fly. When the insects are questing for a spot to lay their eggs, if they land on a number of non-related species among the

Cabbages and fennel growing together: not only are they complementary in looks, but the fennel flowers attract beneficial insects. French marigolds act as a whitefly repellent in glasshouses and tunnels.

brassicas they are likely to deduce that it's not a great place for their young to start their lives, and they fly off elsewhere, looking for a more monocultural patch. The more intermingled the different plants are, the more effective: a chequerboard pattern is better than rows.

Carrot fly can be deterred by onions, but only when the onions are young (not when they are at the bulbing-up stage). Best results in field trials were had when four times the amount of onions as carrots were grown.

The French marigold (*Tagetes patula*) acts as a whitefly repellent in glasshouses and tunnels when it is in flower. I plant it every year in my greenhouse, and the only year we had whitefly was when the young marigold plants were eaten by slugs.

Many other plants are supposed to have deterrent effects on certain pests, but it is hard to know which recommendations are old wives' tales that have been repeated over and over, and which are genuinely useful.

Growing specific plants for beneficial insects is another form of companion planting. Flowering annuals and herbs attract bees and other nectar-drinkers, which pollinate crops. And vegetables of the onion, brassica and carrot families produce flowers that are highly attractive to many different insects, including hoverflies and wasps – both of which are big aphid-eaters. Ground beetles, which dine on molluscs, larvae and aphids, hide in low-growing ground-cover plants such as clover, wild strawberries and hardy geranium. All these create the damp conditions that these shiny ebonite insects like. In our garden, whenever I pull up chickweed or speedwell I find ground beetles. These little weeds are fairly scraggy-looking, but they'll do no harm to vigorous vegetables such as cabbages and beans.

A CRASH COURSE IN THINKING ABOUT VEGETABLES

The world of vegetables is a diverse one. Imagine: a bouncy green pea, a floppy leaf of lettuce and a secretive, underground-dwelling potato must all be considered in the same cluster of plants, just because they are edible. They are as different as can be. Yet for convenience sake they are gathered together here, and in every other gardening book.

Because they are so different, they must be subdivided into categories, but there are countless ways of doing this: by family, by rotational groups, by the conditions they like, by the temperatures they tolerate, by whether they need support or not and so on. The various sets intersect again and again. So for the remainder of this chapter don't be disconcerted when you see the tomato or the bean or any other vegetable belonging to a host of different groups. The more ways you can think of an edible plant, the more you know it and the easier it becomes to grow.

FAMILY MATTERS

All plants are gathered into families, where the members share certain botanical features. They may also share diseases and pests, and have similar requirements regarding nutrition and growing conditions. They may interact with the soil in the same way: for example, all leguminous vegetables have nodules on their roots, which attract beneficial bacteria. These take nitrogen out of the air and make it available in the soil. The similarities are not guaranteed, but it does no harm – and it usually helps – to know what is related to what.

The three families in the kitchen garden of which you need to take most notice are the potato, brassica (or cabbage) and onion clans: *Solanaceae*, *Brassicaceae* and *Alliaceae* – mainly because they are prone to the greatest number of diseases and disorders. In rotations (as discussed above), it's wise not to follow them with their own kind, as pests and pathogens may linger in the soil and attack the new crop. Tomatoes, for example, are the same family as potatoes and equally vulnerable to the devastating potato cyst eelworm. Blight, the historic scourge of Irish potatoes, also affects tomatoes. The spores are airborne, so if your spuds are blighted, keep a good eye on your tomatoes. Edible members of *Solanaceae* also include aubergine, pepper, tomatillo, Cape gooseberry and goji berry. Tobacco is another relative, and although you may not be growing either the smokable or the ornamental kind, cigarettes can be a source of tobacco mosaic virus (TMV), which is indiscriminate about what it attacks. TMV can be passed along by smokers' hands or tools. It seems bizarre that a cigarette can make a tomato sick, but it's true – which is a startling example of why it helps to know your plant families.

The cabbage clan is large. It sprawls from the obvious cabbage, cauliflower, broccoli and kale, through to oriental leaves (pak choi, Chinese mustard, et al.) and on to wallflowers, stock, shepherd's purse, wild mustards and a multitude of other plants. One of the defining features of the family is its four-petalled flowers – which gave it its previous name *Cruciferae*, from the Latin *crucifer*, 'to bear a cross'. All can act as hosts for clubroot. If you are unlucky enough to be visited by this disease (which is related to the slime moulds), it will reveal itself in purple, discoloured foliage and stunted growth. The roots are swollen and disfigured, in such a way that explains its traditional name of 'finger-and-toe'. Liming the soil and providing good drainage (as in raised beds) can help reduce its severity. Growing susceptible plants in small pots – so that they develop a decent root system – before planting them in the soil can also stave it off long enough to achieve a crop. According to the Royal Horticultural Society, the following cultivars have some resistance to clubroot: cabbage 'Kilaxy' and 'Kilaton', calabrese 'Trixie', cauliflower 'Clapton', kale 'Tall Green Curled' and swede 'Marion'.

The onion family is easy to identify and hides no surprise individuals: all its members (garlic, chives, shallots, leeks, etc.) have long, strappy leaves that give off a pungent aroma when crushed. The flowers are composed of numerous little florets, and are attractive to bees and hoverflies. Besides the destructive white rot, other diseases include downy mildew and rust.

The marrow family (*Cucurbitaceae*) includes not just the marrow and its more petite incarnation, the courgette, but cucumbers, squashes, pumpkins and melon. All are tender and will not tolerate frost. They are also all hungry and thirsty plants.

Courgettes belong to the marrow family: all its members are frost tender. Beetroot is related to spinach, chard and orach.

The beet family (*Chenopodiaceae*) takes its botanical name from the Greek words for goose and foot, because the leaf shape in some of its members has a goose-footish look. Alongside beet, it includes spinach, perpetual spinach (also known as spinach beet or leaf beet), chard and orach – all of which are grown for their leaves.

Apiaceae gives us carrots, celery, fennel, parsnip and a host of herbs, including parsley, coriander, dill and lovage. All have the characteristic umbrellas of flowers, which are beloved of bees and other nectar-seeking insects. The underground parts are always taprooted (as in carrots and parsnips).

Lettuce belongs to *Asteraceae*, the daisy family, which may seem unlikely, but if you leave the plants to grow into adults and flower, the knotty little buds transform into minute, clenched-tight yellow daisies. (The slender branched pyramids are beautifully sculptural in the autumn garden.) Other relatives are chicory, cardoon, globe artichoke and Jerusalem artichoke. The family is fairly trouble free, aside from the odd invasion by aphids and the unwelcome attentions of slugs and snails.

The pea family (*Papilionaceae*, formerly *Leguminosae*) takes its name from the Latin word *papilio* for butterfly, because of the shape of the flowers. Most of its kitchen-garden members are obvious: peas and beans, including broad, French and runner beans. If you use green manures, it's useful to know that clover, winter tares (vetch) and alfalfa are also leguminous, and act as nitrogen-fixers.

These are the main families, although there are a few clans that contribute other plants: most herbs are *Lamiaceae*, sweet corn is *Poaceae* and the vast majority of edible fruits belong to the rose family, *Rosaceae*. Asparagus gives its name to the family *Asparagaceae*, a grouping which (and here's an amazing fact with which to end this section) also includes cordyline, lily of the valley and hosta.

TENDER CROPS THAT PREFER COSSETING

It is possible to grow certain food plants outdoors, but to be honest, some of them are a lot happier in a polytunnel, glasshouse or other protected structure. Let's take tomatoes, for example. During a sunny summer, and in a warm part of the garden (against a south-facing wall, ideally), you will get a respectable crop, but in many years the yield will be minimal. Still, if you have no way of growing toms under cover, it's worth trying them outdoors. If the fruits are reluctant to ripen,

Tomatoes do best in a warm sheltered place, such as this polytunnel. The straw mulch conserves moisture and discourages weeds.

harvest them and line them up on a warm windowsill. The British charity Garden Organic recommends the following for outdoor growing: medium-sized 'Alicante' and 'Harbinger', the large 'Marmande' and 'Super Marmande', as well as the cherry tomato 'Gardener's Delight'. In my experience, you need a very hot summer to ripen the mediums and larges, so it may be safer to choose only the small-fruited kinds.

Courgettes are more prolific under glass or plastic, but will give a reasonable crop outdoors in a warm summer. Peppers (both sweet and hot), aubergines, cucumber and melons all need to be grown under protection, unless it is a heatwave year.

If you have room for a greenhouse or polytunnel, do consider putting one in, even if it means you have to cancel your holidays to pay for it. And buy the very largest that you can afford, as the space is so valuable and you'll find so many uses for it (if there is room for a chair and somewhere to rest a cup of tea, all the better). A protected structure doesn't just get warmer than outdoors and allow you to grow tender crops: it also lengthens your season. You can harvest food both earlier and later in the year, as well as giving crops a head start before planting them out in the garden.

HARDY VEGETABLES THAT CAN STAY IN THE GROUND OVER WINTER

Some veg varieties are robust enough in our relatively benign climate to stay in the soil all winter, and to provide us with winter crops or welcome spring treats. My favourite is purple sprouting broccoli, with its nutty, asparagussy flavour, delicate texture and rich colouring. I'm not keen on the Brussels sprout, but if you are, it is a staunch overwinterer. Other brassicas that

will survive the cold season are cabbage, kale and some oriental leaves. All the above, except for the orientals, may need some support to prevent the plants toppling over or being whipped by the wind. Either stake the stems or draw the soil up around them and firm it. Spinach, chard, leeks and autumn-sown broad beans and peas will also overwinter.

PERENNIAL VEGETABLES

Food plants that return year after year seem like a free gift after a while: there is none of the annual slog of sowing, potting on and planting. True, they may need a little grooming and feeding, but the hardest work is getting them into the ground initially. Most perennial vegetables take up a fair amount of space, and may not earn their keep in a smaller garden. If territory is limited, you can try

Purple sprouting broccoli is one of the best-tasting spring crops (and is almost impossible to buy in the shops).

Red-veined sorrel can be grown as a perennial, but the leaves get very bitter if the plants start to bolt (and in truth, they are best when much smaller than the ones shown above).

wild rocket (*Diplotaxis* spp.) and sorrel (*Rumex* spp.), compact leafy plants that last for some years. Use only the young leaves, and shear the clumps back to the base when they become scraggly to get a flush of new tender foliage.

But if you have a larger garden, you can take pleasure in growing perennial vegetables that are difficult to find in the shops, especially from fresh and local sources. The most common are globe artichokes, asparagus, seakale and rhubarb. I know that the last of these is a dessert crop rather than a 'proper' vegetable, but we'll lump it in here anyway.

Globe artichokes, which like a sunny spot and fertile free-draining soil, are ruggedly architectural, with giant, silvery, serrated leaves. In the first year, snip off any flowers as soon as the buds form, so that the energy can be redirected into making a stronger plant. Artichokes crop well for a few years, after which you may need to start new plants from the basal shoots.

Asparagus needs a sunny spot with light to medium soil. The plants can last for twenty years, cropping for six weeks annually. You are not supposed to harvest any shoots in the first year, but it's difficult not to treat yourself to a single stem. Male cultivars, such as 'Glijnlim F1' and 'Theilim', are reputed to be most prolific. The ferny fronds that unfurl from the unharvested spears are quite decorative, but they're functional too, and should be left to feed the roots.

Seakale – as the name suggests – is a seaside plant, so it is happiest in full sun and lightish soil. The young stems are the edible bits, and they must be blanched (left to grow in darkness) first. Cover with a seakale forcing pot or any light-proof container (a large black bucket is ideal) in late winter or early spring, before the shoots emerge. When the pale and elongated stems are about 30 centimetres long (12 inches), cut them at the base. Devoted eaters of the vegetable do not allow the plants to flower, but the little white florets that appear in May and June are honey-scented and edible.

Rhubarb needs plenty of well-rotted manure or other organic matter at planting time. Don't plant too deeply, especially in heavy soil, as the fleshy crowns may rot. Wait until its second year to harvest the stems, and never remove more than half.

CLIMBING VEGETABLES

Food plants that grow upwards save space in the garden, as well as making good-looking arches and pillars of productiveness. Birds, of course, will also be delighted to use these vantage points as song posts. The supporting structure has to be strong and firmly anchored: foliage can be heavy, as can some fruits (squash, cucumber, et al.). And remember that rain and wind will add further stress to the framework. You can use bamboo canes, or rods of ash, chestnut or hazel, as construction materials. Organic gardener and writer Joy Larkcom uses rebar (steel reinforcing rods) covered in chicken wire to make vegetable-clad arches in her garden. Among the crops that you can send skywards are runner beans, climbing French beans, tall peas (most heirloom

Peas scrambling up and around a willow and bamboo fence.

varieties are fairly lofty), cucumbers, courgette ('Black Forest' and 'Black Hawk') and some smaller squash such as 'Red Kuri' and 'Tromboncino'. These marrow family members will need a little help scaling their supports, and will appreciate being tied at intervals, with soft twine. Heavier fruits will also need hammocks: use old mesh vegetable bags or the like.

VEGETABLES THAT TOLERATE DRYISH SOIL

No crop is happy in drought conditions, but there are a few that will put up with soil that is on the dry side. It's important to start them off by adding plenty of water to the planting hole or the sowing trench. This encourages the roots to travel downwards, where the soil is damper and cooler. Don't water them again for a week or more, and when you do, give infrequent but deep drinks rather than lots of little sips, as these evaporate quickly, inducing the roots to stay near the surface. Obviously, mulching when the soil is damp is important. The following crops are more amenable than most to dryish conditions: purple sprouting broccoli, chard, New Zealand spinach (*Tetragonia expansa*), perpetual spinach and wild rocket. *Chenopodium giganteum* 'Magentaspreen' is a towering leafy plant, sometimes known as tree spinach. It can grow as tall as a person, and has jazzy pink and green leaves that can be used in salads. Apparently they can be cooked like spinach also, but you would want a forest of the plants to yield enough bulk for cooking. Most herbs, being Mediterranean species, are also tolerant of dry soil.

FOOD CROPS THAT CAN TAKE A LITTLE SHADE

There are a few edibles that will grow in light shade, as long as there is moisture (but not waterlogging). Dry shade, such as that under conifers, is not suitable for any conventional food plants. However, if you have arid, shady soil that has been invaded by the dreadfully invasive ground elder (*Aegopodium podagraria*), you can take some comfort in the fact that the young foliage is edible. The mature leaves have a laxative effect, so one's nibblings should be confined to springtime. More orthodox edibles that you can plant in moist shade are Jerusalem artichokes, chicory, Chinese leaves, cress, mizuna, radish, sorrel and spinach. The herbs angelica, chervil, mint and parsley are also content in a slightly shady spot. Comfrey, which you can use as a plant food, doesn't mind being denied sunlight.

HUNGRY VEGETABLES

My Minnesota grandfather used to feed his tomatoes with dead fish that washed up on the shores of a nearby lake. The heads and innards of the walleye and largemouth bass that the family had eaten the night before did not go to waste either. My uncle, who was pressed into gardening duties when he was a child, remembers, 'We were told that the Indians used to bury a dead fish with every corn seed that they planted – and that made it less of a burdensome task.'

Should you decide to use fish, do bury it deep enough to discourage animals, and don't put it right next to the roots of a plant, which might expire from too much of a good thing. Although well-rotted manure and garden compost are a lot more congenial, fish decays rapidly and is full of nutrients – and it won't stink up your bin if it's put to good use in the garden.

The relatively new Hungarian-bred 'Sarpo Mira' potatoes: they are more resistant to blight than most other spuds.

The following vegetables do best in fertile, moist ground and may be difficult to grow in light soil: cabbage, Brussels sprouts, courgette, pumpkin, potatoes, spinach, sweetcorn and tomatoes. The last of these need regular watering, as disorders such as splitting skins and blossom end rot can occur when the soil see-saws between moist and dry. Tomatoes are prone to fungal diseases also: you can prevent these spreading by removing any leaves that drag on the ground, and by not wetting the foliage unduly.

POTATOES

I don't have room to cover every vegetable here, but it would be wrong for a garden book that is written in Ireland not to include potatoes. In this country, we like our spuds floury – and so do the Scots. Most of the rest of the world prefers them waxy. In Ireland, the two most popular varieties are the Irish-bred 'Rooster' and 'Kerr's Pink', which was bred in Scotland. Both have high 'dry matter' (as it is known in potato-expert-speak) which means that there is plenty of starch to absorb water as the tuber cooks. When you break open the skin, steam gushes forth and the snowy crystals fluff up and cry out for butter (and perhaps a dash of milk).

Eating a potato is a simple and satisfying thing, but the growing of it seems unfairly complicated by puzzling classifications such as first earlies, second earlies and early and late maincrop, not to mention the fear of blight or other devastating disorders. Rotating your vegetable crops (as discussed earlier) will help keep your spuds healthy, as will choosing less vulnerable varieties. Some of the most exciting of these are the new Sarpo group of potatoes, bred by the Sarvari family in Hungary (the name is a contraction of 'Sarvari' and 'potato'). They are largely blight proof, and have good resistance to slugs, wireworms and viruses. The first year I grew them, which was a very blighty season, the leaves were affected, but the tubers were immaculate. 'Orla' (first early), 'Sante' (early maincrop) and 'Cara' (late maincrop) are some of the others that are fairly stalwart in the face of blight.

And now, before I have to use the terms again, let us demystify this business of early and maincrop potatoes. These categories are determined by the amount of time that elapses between planting the seed potato and harvesting the tubers. First earlies are the quickest to mature, whereas late maincrop varieties take the longest period. The actual amount of time will vary in different areas and in different years, and depends on the climate and conditions. But in general early potatoes are ready to lift after 8 to 15 weeks, and maincrop kinds after 18 to 22 weeks. Earlies yield proportionately smaller crops, are planted closer together and usually do not store well – so they are eaten as new potatoes. Maincrops give high yields and can be kept for some months. If your garden is small and you crave spuds, choose earlies, as you'll be digging them up in late June or July, and you can stick another crop (of a different rotation group) into the soil immediately.

Earlies are traditionally planted early in the season (from mid-March), and maincrops later (from late April and into May). But you don't have to adhere to this rule. You can plant earlies late and maincrops early if you want: the only caveat is that some early varieties are fairly vulnerable to blight. Among those that are dangerously susceptible are 'Duke of York', 'Home Guard', 'Rocket' and the very floury 'Sharpe's Express', so if you are growing these, aim to get them out of the ground as soon as possible. The waxy, Irish-bred 'Orla', mentioned earlier, is one of the most blight-proof first earlies, and it stores well too.

Some gardeners like to 'chit' or sprout their potatoes indoors, in a cool, bright place, such as a porch or spare bedroom: this gives an earlier crop, although it may decrease the yield. Stand the potatoes upright in an egg box or seed tray, with the 'rose' end uppermost. This is the part of the tuber that has the most eyes. (It's a little shocking to discover that a seemingly indeterminate potato has a top and a bottom, but such is the case.) After four to six weeks, when the sprouts are 2–4 centimetres (1–1½ inches), the potatoes may be planted in a trench 15–30 centimetres deep (6–12 inches). Space earlies 30 centimetres (12 inches) apart and maincrops 40 centimetres (16 inches). Cover with a little soil, add some organic matter and then add more soil. When the green leaves appear, mound some soil over them. Do this a couple of times and eventually your trench will grow into a ridge.

I'm all for saving seed, but with this disease-prone crop it's safer to buy certified seed potatoes each year.

At Glebe Gardens these rows of salad plants are continually harvested by picking a few leaves from the outside of each plant every few days.

SALAD LEAVES

The leaf that you raise yourself is a completely different thing from the store-bought item. Not only is it fresher and tastier (picked minutes rather than days earlier), but – if you are gardening without chemicals – it is also free from residues of pesticides, fungicides and herbicides. Pre-washed salad leaves (picked who knows when or where?) are often rinsed in chlorinated water and sealed in polythene bags pumped with 'modified air', a reduced oxygen and increased nitrogen mixture. When you consider the energy expended on this processing and packaging, and on the transport and refrigeration, it may strike you that this is a slightly insane use of the Earth's resources. And, if you want to talk money, bear in mind that for the same price as a 100-gram pack of pre-washed leaves, you can buy a packet of seed that will sprout hundreds of lettuces. It's true that you will have to pick and rinse the leaves yourself, but is that such a chore? Remember, too, that you can recycle the washing water in the garden.

Salads can be squeezed into bits of spare ground in the veg patch, as they are in and out of the soil fairly quickly, and most are not prone to a host of soil-borne pests or diseases. Lettuces are the staples of the salad world: they can be eaten on their own, or used as supporting cast in a bowl of more piquant leaves. No lettuce has a great amount of flavour, but many are

Salad plants find homes in a sturdy wine box and in my friend Grainne's old basket.

charming-looking things, especially the red-leaved varieties – which have the bonus of being less attractive to slugs and snails. The traditional way to harvest most lettuces (although not the looseleaf kinds) is to wait until they heart up and to cut or pull up the whole head. This method gives you tender leaves at the middle of the plant, but there is a lot of waste in the tough and damaged outer parts.

I prefer to harvest the leaves individually when they are between 10 and 20 centimetres (4 and 8 inches) long. I pick only the outer leaves, making sure that the plant retains around six or eight leaves at its centre. During peak growing season, the plants can be revisited every few days, and they will last many weeks before they bolt (run to seed). If you grow your lettuces in a pretty pattern, this method prevents annoying gaps sabotaging your design when you harvest.

Besides lettuce, the following leaves make tasty additions to the salad bowl: beetroot, cabbage, chard, chicory, claytonia (winter purslane), cress, American land cress, leafy herbs (including chervil, coriander, dill, fennel and parsley), kale, lamb's lettuce, orach, onion, summer purslane, radish, turnip, sorrel spinach, perpetual spinach, and oriental greens such as mibuna, mizuna, pak choi, tatsoi and various mustards.

KITCHEN-COUNTER AND WINDOWSILL FARMING

The freshest and fastest crops that a person can raise are sprouts. Not the Brussels variety, but sprouting beans, peas and other seeds. They are the most instant of all home-grown vegetables: you start them on a Saturday and by Wednesday evening they can be on your dinner plate. Mung beans are the most commonly seen commercially available sprouts, but there are crowds of other plants that can be eaten at the embryonic stage – when they are bouncing with nutrition and look interestingly squirmy. Other pea family members that are suitable for sprouting are aduki beans, alfalfa, chickpeas, fenugreek, whole lentils, mung beans and peas. You can also sprout some brassicas: broccoli, cabbage, oriental mustard and radish. Alliums, including chives, garlic chives, leek and onion, are also suitable, but may take up to two weeks to germinate.

Seeds can be sprouted in a large jar: you'll need to fasten a piece of muslin (or nylon stocking) over the mouth with an elastic band. If you become a committed sproutarian (and there is nothing better for banishing the winter blues than witnessing the busy clamour of a throng of germinating seeds), it's worth buying a proper sprouting kit from a health food shop, as this makes the rinsing and draining operation much more efficient.

Sprouts are like Victorian children: they thrive on good hygiene and frequent air circulation. Therefore, the equipment must be clean, and the sprouts must be rinsed and drained regularly.

Puy lentil sprouts: delightfully wriggly-looking, and tasty too.

A sprouter with (from the top) alfalfa, aduki bean and lentil sprouts: each layer must be rinsed thoroughly at least twice a day.

The moist conditions that sprouts require for germination also favour bacteria and fungi. The constant washing and draining prevent these getting a toehold. If your sprouts go slimy or mouldy, turf them out, clean all your equipment and be more obsessive about rinsing and draining next time round.

Sprouts expand dramatically while they are growing – three to ten times the size of the dried seed – so you may need less than you imagine. Throw out any damaged or broken seeds and rinse in cold water. Soak until they have swelled: a few hours, or overnight. Rinse and drain well, so that they are not sitting in any water. Leave them in a warm room, out of direct sunlight: next to the kitchen sink is perfect, as you are not likely to forget them there. Rinse at least twice a day, or more if possible. Taste them each time you rinse, to check that all is well, and to see when to stop growing them. Some seeds – chickpeas, for instance – are tastiest when the sprouts are very small. Other, such as alfalfa, can support more growth. If you dry the sprouts well after their final rinse, they will keep for a few days in the fridge.

Pea shoots are a delicious, gourmet crop that you can grow on the kitchen windowsill at any time of the year. Sow a couple of handfuls of dried marrowfat peas (such as those that are used to make mushy peas) into a tray of potting compost. Space them about 4 centimetres (1½ inches) apart. They will germinate in days. When the shoots are 10 centimetres (4 inches) tall, nip out the tops, tendrils and all, and serve them as a garnish or in a salad. The peas are very productive and will allow you to make half a dozen such harvests before they run out of steam.

FRUIT

Your own home-grown fruit has a magical appeal; harvesting it is a bit like lifting your hand to a tree or bush and plucking a jewel. If your crop is small, chances are that not much of it will make it to the house, and it will end up getting eaten on the spot. It's hard to resist a just-ripened, sun-warmed fruit.

In a large garden, there is plenty of room for as many fruit and nut trees as you like. For tiny

Late raspberries such as 'Autumn Bliss' are easy to manage: prune all the canes to the ground between mid-winter and early spring. In theory one doesn't need to stake them, but ours have always needed support.

gardens, there are tiny apple trees – either columnar types or miniatures grafted on to very dwarfing rootstocks – but the quantity of fruit on these may not be great enough to warrant all the fiddling about that you have to do with the plants. Such trees need very good soil, a fair bit of feeding and staking throughout all their lives. In my experience they are fussy novelty items rather than stalwart larder-fillers. If you are wedded to the idea of growing apples or pears in a small garden, train them on a wall, as espaliers, cordons or fans.

Actually, there is more enjoyment and a lot less bother in growing a small tree or shrub where the berries benefit the birds, rather than providing a token fruit or two for the gardener. Or there is always the possibility of a compromise: grow a crab apple and split the crop between the humans and the avians.

In a smaller garden, try raspberries or currants: they are easier to manage and more compact and prolific. Strawberries, of course, can be grown in the tiniest space, even in a pot. They are one fruit where if you get only a handful, it's worth it.

The year in harvests

Colder gardens or chilly weather produce later or shorter growing seasons; warmer gardens or milder weather may result in earlier and lengthier cropping periods. You can also extend the season at either end by protecting plants with horticultural fleece or a cloche during the first and last days of frost.

- January: winter cabbage, kale, leek, parsnip
- February: sprouting broccoli, winter cabbage, kale, leek, parsnip
- March: sprouting broccoli, winter cabbage, kale, leek, parsnip, salad leaves
- April: sprouting broccoli, leek, radish, salad leaves
- May: sprouting broccoli, carrot, leek, radish, salad leaves
- June: broad bean, French and runner beans, beetroot, summer cabbage, calabrese, carrot, cauliflower, garlic, onions, peas, potatoes, radish, salad leaves, turnip
- July: broad bean, French and runner beans, beetroot, summer cabbage, calabrese, carrot, cauliflower, courgette, garlic, onions, peas, potatoes, radish, salad leaves, sweetcorn, outdoor tomato, turnip
- August: broad bean, French and runner beans, beetroot, summer cabbage, calabrese, carrot, cauliflower, courgette, garlic, peas, onions, potatoes, radish, salad leaves, sweetcorn, outdoor tomato, turnip
- September: French and runner beans, leek, beetroot, summer cabbage, calabrese, carrot, cauliflower, courgette, peas, potatoes, radish, salad leaves, squash, sweetcorn, outdoor tomato, turnip
- October: French and runner beans, leek, parsnip, beetroot, carrot, peas, salad leaves, squash, swede, sweetcorn, turnip
- November: beetroot, winter cabbage, kale, leek, parsnip, swede, turnip
- December: winter cabbage, kale, leek, parsnip, swede
- All year: chard, spinach, some oriental leaves (including mibuna, komatsuna and baby leaf mixtures), herbs. If you have a greenhouse or polytunnel, salad leaves can be harvested year round.

HELPING NATURE GARDEN

'A good Garden may have some Weeds.'
Thomas Fuller, *Gnomologia: Adagies and Proverbs; Wife Sentences and Witty Sayings, Ancient and Modern, Foreign and British*

Gardening with nature is just that, but the emphasis is often on the 'gardening' part. If we don't manage the space outside our door, it stops being a garden, and reverts to being a piece of ground where the most rampant vegetation takes over. And this, although more 'natural', may not actually benefit as large a section of nature. If, for example, a garden with a framework of coniferous shrubs is let 'go wild', the shrubs will eventually shade everything else out, and there will be no flowers for insects or berries for birds. There will also be nowhere for us to sit, play or grow food.

So, an important part of gardening with nature is knowing when to intervene, and having the skill to do it correctly. It's also about using your brain and your eyes. It's about keeping alert and asking questions. You might notice that one end of a row of beans is healthier than the other, and then you might wonder why. Perhaps that area gets more light or more air? Perhaps the level of moisture in the ground is more ideal at the better end? Or maybe the plants there are surreptitiously receiving nutrients leaked from the nearby compost heap?

The more questions you ask of your plants and your plot – as it were – the more answers they will give you. And all the while you are infinitesimally adding to your knowledge as a gardener, until one day you realize that just by paying attention you have taught yourself an awful lot. No one else can *really* teach you to garden. I mean, you can watch, and listen, and read, and go to classes, but you will learn more by just doing it. (Don't worry about making mistakes. There is always next year to do things better.) Along the way, you will develop your own way of doing things, and these might vary a bit from the 'accepted' methods. But that's fine: every garden is different, and so is every gardener.

KEEPING IT HEALTHY
A healthy garden is just like a healthy person: better able to weather disease, stress and other trying circumstances. As I have said elsewhere, one of the keys to a robust and resilient patch

If you forgot to harvest your leeks, let them flower, as here at Dunmore Country School. They attract beneficial insects, and they also look like tennis balls on bendy rods, which is quite happy-making.

Mid-summer garden basket: 'Cavalo Nero' kale, calendula flowers, courgettes and beets, along with my favourite copper trowel and weed grubber. Garden twine, of course, is essential for tying stray bits of plants into place.

is growing what suits your climate and conditions. Another part of the formula – as I also mentioned – is maintaining biodiversity. If you have many different kinds of plants and habitats in your plot, lots of different creatures will visit, and some will make their homes in it. Each living thing in the garden has its place in the network, from the tiniest organisms in the soil, to the insects and other invertebrates that scamper over its surface and live on the vegetation, to the birds that range wherever they want. A diverse community such as this tends to be naturally self-balancing: there are so many things getting eaten by each other that numbers of pests rarely get out of control. It is the opposite of the modern agricultural model of a monoculture, where there are always problems and plagues.

So, although much of the gardener's pest-culling work is already being done by the smaller residents, we still need to maintain vigilance and to take selective action. For example, I keep an eye out for all kinds of plant munchers. If I find a throng of aphids on the nettles at the wild end of the garden, I leave them to get on with their business, knowing that they will feed a generation of fledglings, and the larvae of ladybirds, hoverflies and three native butterflies (small tortoiseshell, peacock and red admiral). But if the aphids are congregating on the buds of one of my few roses, I squidge them off between thumb and forefinger (and wish that I had an 'aphis brush', an implement I've seen in old gardening books – like tongs with soft brushes on the ends).

If you nip potential problems in the bud, you save time and energy, and you don't have to start searching for a remedy. You notice a few spots of powdery mildew on your sweet pea? Immediately remove the dodgy shoots, and if the soil is dry, give the plants a really good soaking at their roots. Stress from lack of water is one of the main causes of this fungus. If you caught the mildew early enough, chances are you've whupped it. The same can be said for many disease, pest and weed nuisances in the garden. Keep your eyes peeled for trouble and, if necessary, take action immediately.

SOIL WELL-BEING AND PLANT NUTRITION

If we look after our soil, we're more than halfway towards a healthy patch. The organic movement's most quoted phrase (and a very good one it is too) is 'Feed the soil, not the plant'. If you build up the soil by adding compost, well-rotted manure or other material as a mulch (and to the hole when planting), your plants will have access to a slow and steady source of nutrition. This is better than dosing them with artificial fertilizers, which can cause sappy growth, making the tissues prone to attack by pests and diseases. Chemically synthesized fertilizers are a bit like junk food for the garden. They add nothing to the soil, except for the specific minerals that they contain. They don't add bulk, or any nutrients that feed the umptillion mini beasts underground. In the long term they can lead to loss of soil fauna, deterioration of soil structure, mineral depletion and other problems. Naturally occurring organic plant foods are a by-product or are renewable (as in manure, compost or comfrey leaves), whereas artificial ones are based on finite resources, and are energy-intensive – with natural gas as one of the principal constituents. If you have even a tiny garden, you can recycle your plant debris in a compost bin. Within six months to a year you will have free, nutritious humus to add to your soil – without even setting foot outside your garden perimeter.

It is possible to overfeed plants by natural means, so don't fall into the trap of thinking that just because something is organic, it's safe to use it willy nilly. Animal manure is particularly nutrient rich, and should be applied where you are expecting a lot of growth, to hungry plants or to build up poor soils. In our garden we generally use it only for roses, clematis and a few other big feeders. Some gardeners don't use manure directly on the soil, but prefer to incorporate it into the compost heap so that it activates and enriches the material there.

Certain soils are naturally fertile, and require just a light mulch of compost to renew their vigour, whereas thinner soils need a heavier load. Vegetable beds are hungrier than other parts of the garden: the constant harvesting of plant material takes a toll on the soil's nutrients, which must be continually replenished. We mulch our little veg beds at least once a year with a 25–50 centimetre (1–2 inch) layer of compost, ideally in autumn as they become empty. It protects the soil in winter, and by spring planting time the worms have hauled most of it below the surface.

Every garden should have some nettles: they are the food plants for three butterflies, and can also be made into a nitrogen-rich plant feed.

Mulching preserves the surface and structure, but soil can also be protected simply by having things growing in it: roots keep it active and leaf cover protects the structure. Green manures are one way of keeping the soil clothed. These are crops such as mustard, buckwheat, alfalfa, rye grass, clover and beans that can be grown for between six weeks and a few months and then dug into the soil. I've had limited experience of them in my garden, as we rarely have bare soil; in addition, we follow a no-dig regime as much as possible, and a crop that must be turned into the soil doesn't fit this idea. Somerset organic gardener and writer Charles Dowding, however, says that field beans or broad beans are suitable for a no-dig system. Because the plants are relatively large, they are easily pulled out of the ground, and you can leave them on the surface until the foliage rots back into the soil or just throw them on to the compost. Mustard can be used as a no-dig green manure, as it is killed by moderate frost and will be dug into the soil for you by the worms. Charles Dowding recommends planting it in August or September.

EMERGENCY TONICS, POTIONS AND POULTICES

If your soil has been given a decent diet of organic material, its plants should have all they need to grow healthily. Occasionally, however, some plants will need a supplementary feed. This might be because the soil is still in its first year or two of being built up with compost and may be lacking balance. Or perhaps you are growing certain food crops, such as tomatoes, which sometimes need a bit of a boost – as do potted plants.

Organic gardeners use many different plant-based lotions and potions, made from nettles, comfrey, dandelion, horsetail (*Equisetum*), burdock, dock and garlic, to name a few. You can, in fact, make a feed out of just about any perennial weed (which is one way of keeping them out of the compost heap), as they all contain valuable minerals that they have sequestered from the soil. I've flirted with several home-made plant concoctions, but I use just nettles and comfrey now, and not even regularly. They are both good stuff. Nettle is high in nitrogen, the element that makes leaves green (and plants too sappy if they get too much). It also contains magnesium, sulphur and iron. Young nettles, from a spring harvest, have the highest concentrations of nutrients. Comfrey is rich in potassium (potash), and also has fair levels of nitrogen and phosphorus.

To make a liquid feed from nettles, steep 1 kilogram of chopped leaves and stems in 10 litres (2.2 gallons) of water. Cover and leave for about two weeks, stirring every few days. Strain the liquid and use diluted, 1 part to 10 parts water. Throw the rotted greenery on to the compost heap.

Comfrey feed is usually made in one of two ways, the first producing a large quantity of ready-to-use liquid and the second a small amount of concentrate. For the first, fill a barrel with leaves, top up with water, cover and leave for four weeks to brew, stirring regularly. Use neat.

To extract the concentrate from the plant, you must make a 'comfrey press', a device where the leaves are compacted under a weight and the resulting liquid is collected. The dark brown juice starts to flow after about ten days, and is used at a 1:20 dilution. The most popular press is fabricated from a length of plastic sewer piping, with a sand-filled plastic bottle as the weight. I won't give you a detailed how-to here, because there are numerous instructions on the Internet. You can also use a layer of comfrey leaves, two or three deep, as a poultice around the base of a plant, or in the trenches and holes when you plant potatoes, tomatoes, beans or other plants. As the leaves rot, they release their nutrients.

Nettle and comfrey liquid are truly revolting smelling, so be careful about splashing them on your clothes or skin. As garden pongs go, their reek is second only to the startling odour of an ancient egg – laid months earlier by a stealthy hen – exploding underneath your foot. Still, as I said, these vegetable-based potions are efficacious when a plant needs a shot of energy. Nettle feed will green up a potted leafy plant (such as basil) when it is looking wan, while comfrey is a useful feed for fruiting plants such as tomatoes, aubergines and peppers. A combination of the two will keep your pots of petunias and other summer lovelies in the pink.

You can also make a nourishing 'tea' by suspending a hessian or polypropylene sack of manure or compost in a large barrel of water. After about ten days, the brew will be ready, but it will be more potent and complex if you leave it longer. Dilute it to the colour of weak tea before using.

Comfrey tea is a nourishing feed for fruiting plants. The cultivar 'Bocking 14' is one of the best kinds as it is sterile and does not set seed.

The roots on this verbena – visible, but not constricted – are at just the right stage for planting out. A young bean plant gets some recycled salad-washing water from the kitchen.

HOW TO PLANT

Shoving a plant into the soil may seem like a simple matter, requiring little thought or preparation. But this little action, which can take less than a minute in the case of small plants, can be the most important sixty seconds in the life of a plant – especially in difficult soils.

If your soil is heavy clay, don't plant anything in it when it is very wet, if possible. Just a few trowel or spade strokes will turn the sodden stuff into the consistency of pottery clay – not the best material for plant roots to penetrate. If you must plant in such conditions, work the soil as little as you can and use a light hand or foot.

Assuming that your soil is nice and workable – not too wet and not too dry – here's how you go about planting (or here's how I do it, and it has served me well over the years). Besides your plant (or plants) and your digging implement, you'll need two buckets, one of water and the other of garden compost. While you are digging the hole, plunge the plant into the bucket of water, so that the compost around the root ball is thoroughly dampened. Dig the hole about the same depth as the plant pot, and a good bit wider. Throw a handful or more of garden compost into the base. Ease the plant out of its container and gently tease the roots out, if they are constricted. If there are weeds growing on the surface of the root ball, peel them away, along with the top centimetre of compost. Place the plant in the hole and fill in, adding more garden compost or other organic material if it is a heavy feeder. Smooth out the soil, and water well to settle the roots.

In very dry soil I vary the method slightly: I water the planting hole thoroughly, filling it up

A mulch of fallen leaves and grass clippings helps retain water and protect the soil in this bed.

several times so that there is a bit of a well in the bottom, place the moist plant in it and pull the dry soil over it to seal the moisture in. I do not water from the top at this point – or indeed for at least a fortnight. The wet soil underneath encourages the roots to grow downwards, making the plants more resistant to drought. An excellent pre-planting root dip is pond mud, the silty stuff that accumulates at the bottom and edges of a garden pool.

HOW TO WATER

I'm fervent about conserving water in the garden, and would never dream of using the hose on the grass, or on most of our ornamental plants. Where possible, we keep our soil mulched or have stuff growing on it, so that evaporation is kept to the minimum. But skimping on water at crucial times is a false economy. Planting time is an important period, so use as much water as necessary at that point. Seedlings are vulnerable too, as they have such tiny root systems. The soil or compost in which they are growing should be lightly moist. But here's a caveat: it's probably easier to overwater seedlings than to underwater them, so don't be too lavish, and always use a fine rose on the watering can or hose. 'Damping off' is a fungal disease that attacks overwatered, overcrowded seedlings; they keel over, looking for all the world as if they are dying for a drink – which is exactly what they don't need.

In the vegetable garden, peas and beans need adequate water while flowering and podding, as do sweetcorn, courgettes, tomatoes, aubergines and other fruit-bearing produce when they are fruiting. Newly planted trees and shrubs may need auxiliary watering during their first year in the ground if the soil dries out. To make sure that the moisture is delivered to the roots, and that it doesn't flow away across the surface, make a low bank of soil around the plant, enclosing the root area. Just scrape the soil into a circular retaining wall a couple of centimetres tall, using a trowel and your gloved hands.

Watering should be done first thing in the morning or in the evening. The latter is usually preferable, as there is no evaporation during the cooler night hours. However, with mollusc-prone plants, evening watering makes the soil lovely and comfy for slugs and snails to slither over during the period when they are most active.

When you are watering, remember that it's the roots that need the moisture. While it's great fun to make lazy arcs and baroque fountains with the hose, and to watch the droplets form rainbows in the sunlight, it can also be a shocking waste of the precious liquid. Water should be applied to the soil at the bases of plants, and not sprayed all over the leaves, where it will evaporate quickly. When you water, be generous, so that the moisture percolates deeply into the soil. It is better to water infrequently and plentifully than frequently and lightly. The latter method causes a plant to make shallow roots, so it becomes less tolerant of drought than a plant with deeper roots that can tap into moisture further down.

NEW PLANTS FROM OLD

Propagating plants is a many-layered delight. It makes me feel godlike, maternal, useful, clever, provident and in tune with nature. Being right at the beginning of a plant's cycle – whether it is a cutting or a seedling – gives me an optimistic glow. I feel hopeful for a bright future for both myself and the scrap of vegetable matter that I'm handling. I like also that I'm performing an age-old task that my mother performed, as her mother did before her and all the mothers before her also. (I realize that's quite a lot of baggage for a single seedling or cutting to carry, but I suspect I'm not the only gardener who feels this way.)

A FEW SIMPLE WAYS TO INCREASE YOUR PLANTS
Division

With herbaceous plants the easiest way to make more is by digging up and dividing them. This works only with clump formers – a category that incorporates a gratifying number of perennials. Among the countless suitable candidates are pulmonaria, hosta, agapanthus, crocosmia, rudbeckia, aster and many ornamental grasses. Spring and autumn are the times for this undertaking. Grasses and more tender perennials fare better if divided in spring, so that the warming soil coaxes them back into growth. If the soil is dry around the plant that you want to divide, water it well first (ideally the day before) so that the tissues are plumped up and ready for the ordeal ahead.

Dig up the plant with as large a root ball as possible. If the central parts are tired and woody, discard them. Get rid of any suspect parts also. The outer shoots are always the more vigorous, as they are the youngest. Split the clump so that there is at least one good shoot with roots per division. The actual splitting can be quite a performance, especially in the case of old and congested specimens. Easier clusters can be divided by hand, with a trowel or with a knife.

Hostas can be divided in spring or autumn, but it is easier in springtime, just when the leaf buds are visible.

But for more recalcitrant masses of roots you will need a sharp spade, a saw or even an axe – and brute force. Try to make clean cuts, rather than hacking away at the same place. The textbook way of dividing plants is to use two garden forks back to back, but which of us has a brace of forks?

A large clump will yield many divisions, which you can pot up and pass on to friends or plant sales. To replant divisions in the ground, fortify the planting hole with a generous amount of garden compost or well-rotted manure. British gardeners could add a sprinkle of bonemeal, which is rich in phosphorus, around the roots, to help them recover. Bonemeal on its own is not available in Ireland, but blood-fish-and-bone, while not an exact substitute, can be used instead. Water well, to allow the soil to settle around the roots. When potting up divisions, add some soil and home-made compost to the planting medium and keep the pots in a shady spot for a day or two to recuperate.

Many spring bulbs that become congested and shy to bloom may also be divided after flowering, when they are 'in the green' – that is, still in leaf.

Another form of propagation that is halfway between division and taking cuttings is the curiously named 'Irishman's cuttings'. This is the time-honoured way that gardeners used to give each other 'slips'. It means to carefully extract a single shoot with a few roots from the side of a plant, without digging it up. Often the slip will be quite small and will need to be potted up and nursed before it is large enough to go into the garden.

Stem cuttings

Cuttings are more likely to succeed if taken in the morning, before the sun has had a chance to draw the moisture out of the plant. However, if you are offered a piece of a coveted plant at any time of the day, take it, and pop it into a plastic bag so that it doesn't dry out. Cuttings don't always 'take', and the reasons are many: they might run out of energy, or suffer a fungal attack from lack of air, or dry out at a crucial point, or not like the time of the year or the weather, or have some other unknown whimsy that you have failed to honour. It's always a race to see which happens first: the rooting or the rotting. The aim is to hasten the first and hinder the second.

The best compost for cuttings is a gritty, free-draining, low-nutrient mixture. I use sieved, peat-free compost with plenty of coarse sand. It should feel scrunchy in your palm when you squeeze it. I don't bother with rooting hormone powder or gel, but some gardeners like to use it.

Stem-tip cuttings

These are made from the non-flowering current season's growth of perennials and shrubs. They may be either 'softwood', where the whole shoot is flexible and young, or 'semi-ripe', where the stem is more adolescent and just beginning to toughen. Dianthus, penstemon, pelargonium (tender geraniums), fuchsia and philadelphus are some of the genera that can be increased in this way. Best results are usually had between late spring and late summer, but you might get lucky any time the plant is in active growth. Choose healthy, non-flowering stems, or stems about to flower (and take off the flower buds). Remove the cutting from the plant by snipping it just above a node (where the leaf joins the stem), about 10–15 centimetres (4–6 inches) down from the shoot tip. Then trim the cutting carefully and cleanly to just underneath the node: the plant's natural growth hormones (auxins) are most active in this area. Strip off the lower leaves and insert the cutting into a pot of moist, gritty compost. If the stem is soft, use a pencil to make a hole for it. Firm the compost snugly around the cutting: rooting is more successful where there is good contact. You can put several cuttings into a pot; leave a couple of thumb-widths between them.

Cover the pot with a hat made from a polythene bag, or a magazine wrapper, to retain moisture. Put in a bright, warm place indoors or in a greenhouse or cold frame – out of direct sunlight. If all goes well, your cuttings will root in a few weeks, and can then be potted on. If any go mouldy, discard them immediately and increase the air flow by cutting the corners off the bag.

Hardwood cuttings

These are one of the great miracles of nature: shove a bare twig in the ground and a year later it will have sprouted roots and leaves and turned into a new plant. Not all shrubs and trees will oblige with this method, but a good number will, especially deciduous kinds that make lots of long, whippy growth in a season. Among them are the coloured-stemmed dogwoods and willows, buddleja, flowering quince (*Chaenomeles*), forsythia, elder and snowberry (*Symphoricarpos*). Old-fashioned and rambling roses can also be propagated in this way. Cuttings can be made any time the plant is dormant, but the best periods are usually immediately after the leaves have fallen in autumn, or just before the buds break in spring. Look for healthy, unblemished, well-ripened shoots that have grown in the most recent season. If you have trouble telling the difference between this year's growth and that from the previous one, run your eye from the stem tip downwards until you find where the wood changes, and becomes noticeably rougher.

Cuttings should be 15–30 centimetres (6–12 inches) long, depending on the spacing of the buds. You can usually make several cuttings from a single stem; just don't use wood that is much thicker than a pencil. Trim the bottom of each cutting underneath a node using a straight cut and make a slanting cut at the top, above a bud and sloping away from the bud so that rainwater runs away from it. The different angles on either end will also prevent your inserting the cutting head first into the soil. If you have light soil, you can just plunge the cuttings into a sheltered bed where they won't be disturbed, leaving about a third of the length above ground. If you have heavier soil, add lots of grit or coarse sand first. The rooted cuttings will be ready to lift and pot up in a year.

SOWING SEED

Nature's abbreviation of a future plant into a single seed is one of the many sensational incidents along the cycle of germination, growth, flower production, seed making and dispersal. And although I've sown hundreds of thousands of seeds in my several decades as a gardener, I still get an anticipatory thrill each time I set this cycle off again by placing the perfect parcel of genetic matter that is a seed into a container of compost.

You will probably develop your own way of sowing seeds in time, but until then, let the seed packet guide you on essentials such as when to sow, the ideal temperature, the depth and the spacing. Also, because seedlings are vulnerable little things, be mindful of hygiene. If you are not sowing directly into the ground, use clean containers, fresh compost and clean water. After use, wash out the containers with hot water and soap to kill any possible pathogens, dry them and store in a clean, dry place so that they are ready to go the next time you need them.

You can buy special seed compost or use aged, sieved leafmould, if you have it (but make sure that it does not contain weed seeds); or you can mix your own sowing medium. I use the same mixture for seeds as I do for cuttings: a combination of sieved peat-free compost and

Penstemon is easily propagated from stem-tip cuttings. Chard seedlings push up from seed modules.

horticultural sand, with the latter making up 25 to 50 per cent of the blend. Larger seeds can be sown individually in pots, whereas smaller ones can go into shallow pots or half-size seed trays – full-size trays are usually too large for a single gardener's needs. Or, as I mentioned in Chapter 2, you can re-use the plastic trays from vegetables and other foods that you buy at the supermarket. Choose sturdy containers, 4–8 centimetres (1½–3 inches) deep, and poke holes in the bottom for drainage. You can also use seed modules – plastic trays with individual cells into which you can put one or two seeds. These keep the root balls intact so that the plantlets get less of a fright when you move them on into pots or into the garden.

Fill your container of choice with compost, and water it with a gentle spray: a watering can with a fine rose is perfect. Some gardeners like to place the container in a basin of water and let the moisture seep in from the bottom, but this can make the compost too soggy. Sow the seeds evenly and sparsely. Don't pour them straight from the seed packet, even though you may see this method used on gardening television: it is a surefire recipe for your seeds to end up in a heap at one end. Instead, pour a few into your palm and, with your thumb and forefinger, gently drop them on to the compost. Cover with a fine layer of compost at the depth recommended on the package: smaller seeds have less energy, so should be sown more shallowly. I like to top off my seed trays and modules with a very fine layer of coarse sand; this helps retain moisture

Beetroot seeds can be sown directly into the ground, or the seedlings may be transplanted when they are very young, as here.

and stops algae from forming on the surface. Water again if necessary and put the container in a propagator or a polythene bag, leaving some air space at the top. This allows it to recycle the moisture, and makes a congenial environment for sprouting.

Seeds that require warmth to germinate can be placed on a sunny windowsill or near a radiator, or you can use a heated propagator. As soon as they sprout, they should be moved to a bright place, so that they don't grow lanky and wan while searching for the light.

Seedlings are ready to be potted on into separate containers when they have grown their first set of true leaves. Most seedlings produce a pair of cotyledons initially. These are embryonic leaves that differ in shape and texture from the true leaves. If you sow single seeds in modules, the plants can stay a little longer before going into pots or into the ground. But don't leave plants in small containers for too long: as soon as the roots peep out of the bottom, they are ready to move on.

SAVING SEED

Collecting seed one year, carefully storing it and sowing it the following season is one of the more ancient tasks performed by humans. For our ancestors, saved seed meant the difference between living and starving. For gardeners today, seed saving isn't critical, but it is satisfying. It

Home-saved runner bean seeds: if you have too many for the garden, use them in stews or soups.

positions us at that important lull in the seasonal cycle of death and rebirth, when new life has been secured and waits quietly inside the seed. It also allows us to preserve old or special strains of plants, or to improve on existing varieties by saving the seed of only the plants that exhibit certain desirable characteristics. For example, we can choose to save seed from individuals that are more drought-proof, or more resistant to mildew, or less interesting to insects than other plants in the same batch. Or we might select for flower colour or size, or for a plant that is taller or smaller, bushier or leaner, earlier or later.

There are innumerable qualities (alone and in combination) that a seed saver or backyard breeder might bear in mind while deciding which plant's genes are worth preserving. After a period of selection, the divergence from the original plant can be remarkable. Consider, for example, the case of *Brassica oleracea*, the wild cabbage. A couple of thousand years ago, growers started selecting plants with larger and more succulent leaves, and bred only from them. By around the fifth century BC, kale had been developed; a few hundred years later, cabbage and kohl rabi were established, by more selective seed saving. Over the ensuing centuries cauliflower, broccoli and Brussels sprouts were all bred by selection. The wild mother species of all of them is edible and nourishing, but the leaves are a mere mouthful compared to, say, the massive elephant ears produced by the cabbages of today. In other ways the Mediterranean *mater familias* is very different from her vastly modified descendants.

So, while we're unlikely to create a new brassica category in our vegetable plots, we can still make small changes over time to a plant variety so that it becomes adapted to the conditions of our plot or pleasing in some other way. Or we can simply save seed to keep heirloom plants or choice varieties in circulation. Saving seed, of course, costs nothing, and can cut the seed-buying bill the following year.

Not all plants produce seed that is suitable for saving. F1 hybrids are a case in point. These are the first generation of crosses (F1 means first filial cross) made by seed companies, using two distinct parental lines – in the same way that a horse and a donkey are bred to produce a mule. If you save seed from F1 hybrids, the offspring may not resemble the parents, or the plants may be sterile (as are most mules, as it happens). If you are planning on saving your own vegetable seed, be aware that many modern vegetable varieties are F1s. Instead, look for varieties that are described as open pollinated, heirloom, landrace or traditional.

Next, you must ascertain if the plant is a self-pollinating variety, or if it uses the wind or an insect to ferry its pollen to another plant of the same species. Self-pollinators are the easiest kinds from which to save seed, as there is little risk of their crossing with other, related plants. Most tomatoes are self-fertile, and an investigation of their flower forms will show you why. The stamens (the male, pollen-bearing parts) are clenched in a cone around the stigma (the female bit), protecting it from pollen from an outsider. However, the occasional tomato variety – some beefsteak and potato-leaved kinds, for example – has a protruding stigma, so with the help of a passing insect, the flower can mate with other tomato varieties that you may be growing.

Basic botany is essential for gardeners, and I owe my own knowledge to the frightening biology teacher who regularly intimidated me and my eleven-year-old classmates. I can still feel our combined mortification the morning she bellowed: 'Now, girls, we are going to talk

More tomatoes

Saving tomato seed is fiddly, but fun in a science-project way. Cut the fruit in half and scoop out the seeds with the surrounding jelly-like liquid. Put in an open container, add a little water and leave in a warm place – the airing cupboard will do nicely. Swirl around a couple times a day, if you remember. The mixture will ferment, which breaks down the gelatinous coating on the seeds and also prevents bacterial infection. After about three days, a pad of mould will form on the surface. Don't be alarmed: this is part of the plan; it means that the seeds are ready. Throw the fungal capping away, and fill the container with warm water. Viable seeds will sink to the bottom. Pour off the pulp and liquid. Keep refilling and pouring until only the good seeds remain. Strain them into a sieve, rinse well and leave to dry on a plate for a couple of days. When completely dry, gently scrape them off the plate and seal in an airtight container.

Bolting lettuce plants, about to come into flower. Keep your secateurs sharp and clean so that they cut smoothly through wood.

about *sexual reproduction'* – pause to register our embarrassment – 'in plants!' She's pushing up the daisies now (with their disc florets and ray florets – 'they are not just *petals*, girls'), but I can't say 'stamen', 'anther', 'stigma' or 'ovary' without remembering her and cringing a little.

Lettuce is self-pollinating, so it is safe to grow more than one kind, and to collect the seed. Let the plants bolt and flower, and as the seed ripens, gently shake it free into a paper bag or over a tray. You can safely save the seed of beans and peas also, as the pollen is normally transferred from anther to stigma before the flower opens for business. Leave the pods to dry on the plant; when they are brown and papery you can harvest them. In wet weather, pull up the whole plant at the end of the season, and hang it up to dry in an airy place.

Vegetable crops other than those above are liable to cross-pollinate with related plants, and to get their genes all mixed up. Brassicas, such as the motley crew of *B. oleracea* that I talked about above, will readily cross with each other. So also will marrows, courgettes and certain squashes, as these are all variations of *Cucurbita pepo*. Bees can carry pollen from another vegetable patch half a kilometre away, so there are plenty of possibilities for misbegotten offspring. All insect-pollinated crops are tricky to keep pure: seed saving requires strategies such as isolating blocks of plants or tying bags over the blooms after hand pollinating. Wind-pollinated crops, such as chard, beet and spinach, can also be problematic. I don't mean to be discouraging (because seed saving is such a rewarding task), just realistic. If you fancy the idea of saving seed, start with the easy stuff and see how you like it.

When selecting plants from which to collect seed, keep an eye out for interesting or worthy traits that you would like to develop or foster, and choose only the most healthy and disease-resistant specimens.

PRUNING: A PRIMER

Pruning strikes fear into the heart of some gardeners, and they are afraid to touch anything lest it goes all wrong. Others are completely unfazed, and commit appalling crimes of plant butchery without even knowing it. The remedy for both of the above situations is knowledge. If you understand the process that the secateurs or saw initiates in the plant, you're on the road to many years of happy and effective pruning.

Pruning, quite simply, makes things grow. Yes, it's true that it makes them smaller immediately after you've lopped a few bits and pieces off, but in a little time, it promotes growth. If you remove a branch, twig or shoot from any kind of plant, it usually produces several in its place. The reason for this is 'apical dominance': one of my very favourite (and brainy-sounding) terms in gardening.

Apical dominance

The bud at the end of a shoot (the apex) is like a despot in command of the branch or stem. It sends hormones down to the buds below to inhibit them from developing, and so ensures that it maintains its position as the most assertive and vigorous part of that particular stem. No other shoot is given a chance to surpass it. Spruce and fir Christmas trees, with their triangular shapes presided over by a leading shoot, are perfect illustrations of apical dominance.

When a gardener (or an animal or a bout of frost) comes along and snips off the end of the stem with the chief bud, the oppressing mechanism is disrupted. The lower buds – which have been sitting quietly (and invisibly, in some cases) – suddenly receive a message to grow, and off they go. Anyone who has ever grown a geranium on the windowsill and pinched out the tips to make the plant bushier knows about apical dominance already, even if they can't put a name to it.

So the worst kind of pruning is where someone takes a secateurs to a too large tree or shrub and snip-snip-snips busily at the outer bits until it fits into its allotted space. In a year, the thing has turned into a bristling hedgehog, thanks to all the energy that has been unblocked by the beheading of the leading shoots. If you're trying to create a hedge, this is the way to go about it. But if you want to retain the graceful branchwork of a tree or shrub, you should cut individual stems or branches as far back as possible: to the base, to the trunk or to a main branch.

The reason why

The main effect of pruning is to promote growth, as we've just discussed. But the reasons for setting about a tree or shrub with a pruning implement may be several. It might be to mould it into shape (as with hedging or topiary); or to remove dead or diseased parts; or to take out

You can't put the pruned bits back on the plant, so think twice before snipping.

tired, old wood that has lost its enthusiasm for flowering or fruiting. Or it might be to let air and light into the centre of a fruit tree; or perhaps to promote a flush of new, bright growth in coloured-stemmed willows and dogwoods.

When you know what you're hoping to achieve, and are armed with a few facts, your pruning adventures are more likely to have a successful outcome.

Useful things to know

- Because pruning makes things grow, you need to do it regularly. Some plants grow faster than others. If you are spending an inordinate amount of time keeping a shrub or tree in check, it might be a good idea to cut your losses and plant a less vigorous or more compact specimen.
- Tools for pruning should be sharp and clean. A blunt tool is dangerous to you, and to the plant also, as it leaves ragged cuts that welcome disease.
- You can't put pruned branches back on to a tree, so do stand back and consider what you are doing every couple of minutes.
- Dead, diseased and damaged stems and branches should be cut out first, as the gaps they leave may dictate which other branches should be removed.

Philadelphus 'Belle Étoile' blooms on the previous year's growth, so prune it in summer, when flowering finishes.

- When reducing the length of stems, prune back to just above a healthy bud that is facing the direction you want the new stem to grow (usually outwards). Slope the pruning cut away from the bud so that rainwater doesn't run into it.
- Some flowering shrubs make their blooms on the previous year's growth, some on the current year's. Philadelphus, weigela and deutzia flower on wood made the previous year, and should be pruned immediately after flowering in summer. Hydrangea and buddleja flower on new wood and should be pruned in spring.
- Deciduous trees should be pruned in winter when they are dormant, except for the *Prunus* genus, which are prone to silverleaf disease if winter pruned. These should be attended to in summer instead.
- Most conifers (including Leyland's cypress) hate hard pruning. If they have become too large, do not cut back to the bare trunks, unless you want naked, wooden limbs. Juniper, yew and *Thuja* are the exceptions and will produce fresh shoots from bare wood.

GARDENERS' GOLD: HOME-MADE COMPOST

'Shall I not have intelligence with the earth? Am I not partly leaves and vegetable mould myself?'
Henry David Thoreau, *Solitude*

Sometimes when I talk about the benefits of home-made compost I feel like a quack peddling snake oil. But it is the most fantastic stuff, and the cure for so many afflictions in the garden. Allow me to give you my pro-compost sales patter for just a minute of your valuable time.

Are you suffering from dry soil? What you need is compost, to retain water and add bulk. Or perhaps your soil is heavy and wet? Then why not try compost to open up the texture and help with drainage? Or is your soil tired, lacklustre and uninterested in life? Just give it some compost, and the micro-organisms will colonize it and give it new vigour, and earthworms – attracted to the organic morsels – will arrive and get to work improving the structure. Do you want to get your trees, shrubs, climbers and perennials off to a good start in life? Add compost to the planting hole. Are your roses and fruit bushes feeling unnerved after a pruning session? Give them a healing blanket of compost to set them back on their feet. And what about that lawn that is looking thin and wan? Add a layer of fine compost 1 centimetre (0.4 inch) deep, brush it over the surface and let the worms do the rest. Within four weeks the magical compost will have breathed new life into your grass, perking it up and greening it up.

Compost, as you have probably now gathered, is the elixir of life, a superfood for gardens, stimulating, feeding and bulking up soil. It can also make plants less susceptible to disease. If you add one tenth (or more) of sieved compost to the commercial potting medium you use in your containers, the plants will be less prone to soil-borne diseases. Researchers have found that the beneficial micro-organisms in the compost compete with the pathogens, and suppress their growth.

Compost can also inhibit foliar diseases if applied as a spray: again, the microbes in the compost leave no room for the pathogens to multiply. Soak 1 part mature compost in 10 parts water and leave for ten days, stirring a couple of times daily. Then dilute with 10 parts water, strain and spray on the leaves of your tomatoes or other vulnerable plants. Spray weekly (and after heavy rain) *before* you see any signs of trouble, making sure that you thoroughly drench

May we interest you in some compost? This is the magic solution for whatever ails your garden.

the leaves, including the undersides. If you suspect that the leaves are already infected, spray on three consecutive days and then weekly. The efficacy is variable, and depends on what micro-organisms are present in the liquid. Compost spray is not a registered fungicide, so strictly speaking, one should not use it as such. However, it is perfectly fine to use it as a foliar feed, and if it happens to lock out some fungal invaders in the process, well, isn't that a bonus?

COMPOST JUST HAPPENS

There are as many ways of making compost as there are of baking bread. Every gardener I know has a different method – and each one staunchly defends their procedure as the very best possible. But the fact is that dead matter *wants* to decay: composting just speeds up the operation and manages it. If you do nothing more than fling all your garden waste into a corner, it will eventually decompose. Nature breaks down the tissues of all life forms as soon as they have perished, and eventually recycles them into soil. Otherwise there would be no room on the planet for new life, as the earth's surface would be layered sky high with perfectly preserved dead things.

When we pile our compostables into a heap or container in an organized manner, the decaying process is hotter and more thorough, so that weed seeds and diseases are killed. If you have a very large garden and create a lot of green waste, an open heap or a windrow (an elongated loaf shape) is an option. But most domestic gardeners do not have enough space and will be looking for a tidier operation, such as a composting container. There are dozens of kinds that you might use: home-made affairs fashioned from corrugated metal, bricks, blocks, wire mesh, recycled pallets or other timber; or manufactured items of wood, plastic or metal. Composting has never been more popular, and there have never been more containers and accessories on the market. There are composters that are conical, tubular and square, and there are those that are shaped like beehives and space pods. There are rotating cylinders that look like the barrels for twirling raffle tickets before the big draw. There is even a sphere that you can roll around the garden like a giant basketball to aerate the stuff that is decomposing inside.

All will make you compost sooner or later. In my experience the best compost is made when the heap or container is about 90 centimetres (36 inches) or more wide. This volume is sufficiently large to build up and retain enough warmth so that most weed seeds are killed.

THE COMPOSTING PROCESS

When you pile your compostables into your bin, or on your heap, nature sets to work immediately. Mesophilic bacteria, which live at temperatures between 10 and 40°C (50 and 104°F), are the first to move in and multiply while consuming the material that is most readily broken down (sappy green leaves, grass clippings and manure). As this nitrogen-rich matter degrades, it releases heat, and the compost begins to steam, often within hours (a most satisfying sight). When the temperature rises to over 40°C (104°F), it gets too hot for the mesophiles, and the next crew moves in: the thermophilic bacteria. These tiny microbes swarm all over the remaining material, causing much of it to disintegrate into humus and carbon dioxide. If your

Grass clippings, leaves and weeds from the garden: this time next year all this will be nutritious compost.

heap has the right amount of air and moisture, the temperature during this phase is usually high enough (55–68°C/131–154°F)) to kill weed seeds, as well as plant and animal pathogens.

When the heat cools, the next bunch of compost workers arrives: more bacteria, fungi, protozoa, rotifers and other miniature beings. Finally larger creatures, such as woodlice, millipedes, detritus-eating slugs and red brandling worms move in for the closing stages of the operation. When the brandlings (which are thinner and more wrigglesome than earthworms) retreat to the bottom of the pile, you know your compost is ready. To my mind, this tremendously busy cycle, with its miniature universe of creatures all working together, is one of the most exciting things that a gardener can witness and play a part in.

THE INGREDIENTS

If you want your garden debris to go through all the exhilarating stages above, and to emerge at the end as crumbly, moist compost, you'll need to loosely follow a rough recipe. Making compost is akin to making a wholesome country soup. As long as you get the basics right, you can improvise with what goes in and how you treat it. The end result is always nourishing and delicious.

Almost anything that once grew in the garden can be composted. However, when you are starting out, it's best not to include diseased plants, weed seeds or the roots of persistent perennial weeds such as bindweed, dandelion and ground elder. Leave them in the sun to dry out thoroughly, which may take several weeks, or 'stew' them in a bucket of water for two months and use the liquid to water your plants. Clippings of conifers and yew, and of plants with waxy leaves, such as laurel, holly and ivy, take a long time to break down. If you have room, you can compost them separately (with grass clippings to speed up the process), or you can send them off to your local green waste facility. Do not put plant matter that has been treated with chemicals into your compost.

Along with garden debris, you can compost newspaper (in moderation), brown cardboard, paper towels, hair, wool, wood ash and the contents of your vacuum cleaner, if you don't have synthetic carpets that shed fibres. The litter from rabbits, guinea pigs and poultry can also go into the bin. The latter is very high in nitrogen, and is good for firing up the composting process. Kitchen waste can also be composted, but do not include cooked food or animal products (although eggshells are fine), as these will attract vermin. Indeed, fruit and vegetable

Vegetable scraps, coffee grounds and egg shells are all fodder for the compost heap.

Grass clippings are full of nitrogen and are considered 'green' material for the compost mix.

peelings may attract rats anyway, so don't leave them lying around on top of a heap or uncovered bin.

For simplicity's sake, compostable material can be categorized as either 'green' or 'brown'. The first is nitrogen-rich and is quick to rot down: this is what activates the cycle and gets the heat going. The second is more carbon heavy and slower to decay, and is what gives finished compost its bulk. 'Green' materials include grass cuttings, soft green weeds and herbaceous matter, nettles, comfrey, kitchen waste, seaweed and poultry manure. 'Brown' stuff includes dried plant matter, autumn leaves, eggshells, fine hedge clippings, straw, hay, newspaper and cardboard.

AND SO TO COOK

A mixture of two or three parts green to one part brown will give you perfect compost in most situations. In an ideal world, you build a heap or fill the container all in one session, as a larger quantity of material heats up more quickly than a smaller one. Start with a layer of open, twiggy stuff at the bottom, to give the pile a cushion of air to draw upon. Lay this on the soil, so that worms and other invertebrates can make their way up. Then add your well-mixed greens and browns. Browns should be chopped as small as possible, as they decompose more quickly when a greater surface area is exposed to air, moisture and organisms. If you have a large quantity you could consider buying or hiring a shredder.

Some gardeners like to layer different materials on top of each other, and to incorporate bands of soil, but this is unnecessarily complicated for a backyard operation. Soil is useful because it contains micro-organisms, but there is usually enough adhering to the roots of the plants in the mix. Compost (either finished or not) from an earlier operation can also be added.

When you have built the pile, water it, unless there is lots of wet material in it already. Cover with a lid, a piece of old carpet or even cardboard, to keep it warm. After a couple of weeks, or any time thereafter, you can turn the heap, making sure that the less decayed stuff on the outside is in the middle. This incorporates more air, and starts another cycle of activity. At this point, check to see if it needs more greens, browns or water. Moisture is essential because the microbes live in the films of water surrounding the particles of composting organic matter. (Water and air are as crucial as the actual material in this process.) Depending on the time of

What's wrong with my compost?

Home-made compost doesn't always turn out exactly as you imagine it will. But, fortunately, its problems are usually easily solved.

Bad smells

Why: Excess moisture or not enough air. You may be adding too much kitchen waste or cut grass.

Fix: Turn contents out of bin or heap and rebuild with more browns. Use crumpled, torn-up newspaper or cardboard if you have nothing usable in the garden.

Material just sitting there and not breaking down

Why: Not enough greens, or water, or warmth.

Fix: Remake the pile, adding grass clippings or other greens. Add water if it seems dry. If the weather is very cold, wait until it warms up before giving it more greens. If there is still no activity, proceed as above. Urine is one of the best and most readily available nitrogenous activators for slow heaps. Since Roman times, writers on matters horticultural have recommended that workers pee into composting matter.

Flies

Why: Too much kitchen waste or other attractive rotting matter.

Fix: Make sure the balance is right (see above) and don't leave kitchen waste in the top layer. Make sure there is no meat, fish or food matter in the pile. Cover the surface with a layer of dry material or soil.

Spiders, centipedes, black beetles, enormous slugs and other scary creatures

Why: The faster-moving invertebrates are usually preying on the slower creatures living in the compost. The slugs are probably *Arion ater*, a species that is more interested in decaying plants than live ones.

Fix: Don't worry. Be happy. This is how it's supposed to be.

Rats and mice

Why: They are looking for something to eat or a warm place to hang out.

Fix: Don't add cooked foods, fats or animal or dairy matter to the pile. Use a closed bin and cover the ground at the base with sturdy wire mesh. Bend it up around the outside of the container. Rats and mice are all around us, and you may need to take mortal action with traps, terriers or poison (be very careful with the last). Site your composting station away from the house and always wear gloves when you are attending to it.

the year and other factors, the compost will be ready after six to twelve months. In our garden, we usually let it cure for another six or more months before using.

If you cannot build a heap all in one go (and how many of us have enough garden waste to do so?), you can stockpile your browns indefinitely. Greens start to decay immediately and can be stored for only a limited time. If you are filling a container or building a pile piecemeal, try to gather together enough material to make at least a 40-centimetre (16-inch) layer. This will generate some heat, and is much better than throwing on little dribs and drabs of compostables. My problem is often not having enough green stuff – as our grassed area is relatively small – but we have been lucky to have a series of neighbours next door who are happy to donate their lawn mowings. If you compost other people's garden debris, make sure that it has not been treated with pesticides or weed killers.

LEAFMOULD

If your garden produces only a few autumn leaves, it's best to put them into the compost heap. But if you have a lot, you can make lovely leafmould, a deluxe and much sought after substance. It is slim on nutrients but makes an excellent soil conditioner, because it retains water and contains beneficial microbes. On its own, or after a secondary composting with comfrey leaves, it can be used as a seed-sowing medium. It is also used as an ingredient in superior home-made potting composts. Certain competitive gardeners who grow woodlanders, such as trilliums and the posher primulas, will do anything to get their hands on the stuff. If they don't have any themselves, they won't think twice about plundering nature's own leafmould from woodlands – which is not something I recommend. (These are often the same genteel bandits into whose handbags choice plants just happen to drop when they are visiting other people's gardens.)

Nothing could be easier than making leafmould. All you need are leaves, time and gentle moisture. The decomposition mechanism is a cool one, relying mainly on fungi rather than bacteria. Potting-compost-ready leafmould takes about two years to decay. Just gather your leaves, preferably when damp, and shove them into a wire cage (which is easily made by banging four posts into the ground and surrounding them with chicken wire). Water the leaves if they dry out. And wait.

Beech, hornbeam and oak make the finest leafmould. Larger leaves, such as chestnut, sycamore and plane, take longer to decay: you might like to run the mower over them to shred them first. The accompanying grass clippings will speed up the process and may add a little nitrogen to the product. Evergreen leaves are not suitable, and are better added to the compost heap, after mowing over or otherwise shredding them. Pine needles can be placed in a separate container, where they will make an acidic leafmould.

Leafmould can also be made in a black plastic sack – which can be left to sit quietly in a corner of the garden. Just cram damp leaves in, tie the top and then harpoon it several times with a garden fork, to make air holes. The plastic keeps the leaves moist and the harpooning action is very therapeutic for the gardener.

A wormery, where worms turn kitchen waste into rich compost; and compost worms.

WORM COMPOSTING

This is an appealing technique where a colony of brandling worms (also known as tiger worms) lives in a container and chomps through your kitchen waste, turning it into high-nutrient compost and liquid feed. Running a wormery (or vermicomposting, which sounds more serious) can be tricky for beginners, as it takes a while to learn the ways of the wriggling workers. You must feed the worms little and often, and not overtax their digestive systems with orange peel, dairy products and various other foods. My own efforts at worm farming took place in a home-made worm bin, but I gave up after about a year. Ants invaded the container and it soon became unclear whether I was rearing them or the worms. Nowadays, though, you can buy enclosed wormeries, which keep the worms inside and the ants outside. I'm a little envious of those who have mastered the art of worm husbandry; they always seem to have a warm relationship with their worm herds, and they take great pleasure in overseeing the operation.

THE PROBLEM WITH PEAT

Peat is a non-renewable resource. Or rather, it regenerates by about 1 millimetre per year, but commercial extraction is running at over 200 times that rate. Peat bogs are specialized habitats

An Irish bog has its own specialized fauna and flora (including bog cotton, seen here).

with their own flora and fauna, including several endangered species. The bogs also play a part in regulating water supply and quality. They act as giant sponges, mopping up water during wet periods (which helps to prevent floods) and releasing it back into the atmosphere in drier times. Amazingly, 10 per cent of the planet's fresh water is held in bogs. Carbon is also locked away in their fabric, and is emitted when peat is harvested, contributing to climate change.

But despite the fact that it is a dwindling resource, most commercial 'multi-purpose' composts are made from peat. Since the 1960s Irish peat has been marketed widely for its horticultural uses. It is in demand in western Europe. We extract 2.5 million cubic metres from our bogs per year for gardening purposes, and send 90 per cent of that abroad. Peat is a sterile, lightweight, attractively coloured, water-retaining and easily controllable material. It's not surprising that it stole the hearts of nurserymen and gardeners. But when you think about it, it is madness to continue using it, now that we know how important peat bogs are. It's madness too, when the world is piling up with organic material that can be recycled into potting compost – either in your own back garden or by a commercial venture.

It's true that the technology of peat-free composts is still in its infancy, but it will progress at a faster pace if more gardeners demand alternatives to peat. At present, non-peat composts are made from recycled plant waste, coir (coconut fibre), wood products and other organic residue. Some are twice the price of peat, but this is not surprising, as they have to go through the actual composting process. Peat, on the other hand, has already been rotted down by nature over several thousand years and needs only to be ripped from the earth, milled, mixed with a few additives and packaged.

Proprietary peat-free composts behave differently from peat when used in containers, so they can take some getting used to. For example, the surface of the compost might be dry, even though there is adequate moisture underneath. Some non-peat composts are coarse and need to be sieved for certain plants. It's not uncommon for gardeners to just give up when they run into such difficulties, and to go back to using peat-based products. I've had my own problems with peat alternatives – fungus flies and sinking compost levels, to mention two – but I'm happy to put up with a bit of nuisance while these more earth-friendly composts are being developed.

MOVING AWAY FROM PEAT

Even if you can't imagine a gardening life without peat, you can reduce your use of it. Commercial soil-based composts, such as the well-known mixes formulated by the John Innes Institute, do contain peat, but it is not the main ingredient. John Innes Nos 1, 2 and 3 composts contain 7 parts loam, 3 parts peat, 2 parts sand or grit and varying amounts of fertilizer additives. John Innes composts have more resilience than all-peat kinds, and give much better results with plants that live in containers for long periods of time.

Remember also that you can use your own garden compost in containers. It's generally too rich to use on its own, but you can mix it with commercial compost for a nutritious potting medium. We grow all our containerized vegetables (peppers, aubergines, etc.) and summer flowers in a mix of equal parts home-made compost and bought-in peat-free compost. To reduce the number of weeds that appear from seeds lurking in our own compost, we top off every pot with a 5-centimetre (2-inch) layer of bought-in stuff.

YOUR OWN POTTING COMPOST

Or you can go the whole hog and make your own potting medium. There are hundreds of recipes (you will find them all over the Internet), with different ingredients for different kinds of plants. Just remember to sieve the various components if they are coarse, and to mix everything very well.

Here's one that you might like to try on your potted flowery things: 'four barrowfuls of loam, steeped in night-soil and urine; two barrowfuls of goose-dung, mixed with blood; two barrowfuls of sugar-bakers' scum; and two pecks of sea-sand'. This comes courtesy of London florist Isaac Emmerton, who used this interesting blend for growing auriculas during the early nineteenth century. His raw materials were considered unnecessarily noisome by one of his contemporaries, Thomas Hogg, who wrote in the first volume of *The Magazine of Botany and Gardening, British and Foreign* (1833): 'The ingredients which he recommended, for the most part, are of a nature too filthy and offensive for general adoption, as well as too tedious in

A well-matured two-year-old sample of my own vintage garden compost, sieved.

preparation . . .' Emmerton, apparently, was wont to say, 'My father used them and I used them after him, and made improvements upon them, and nobody grew Auriculas better' – which suggests that his recipe was not the only thing tedious about him.

So instead, let me commend to you these compost recipes from Garden Organic (the British organic organization), which will offend no one, I hope:

- For seedlings: mature leafmould on its own; or equal parts leafmould and loam
- For potting on: equal parts loam, garden compost and leafmould; or 2 parts leafmould or peat-free compost, 1 part grit, 3 parts loam and half a part of garden compost
- For long-term growing: 4 parts loam and 2 parts leafmould; or 3 parts loam, 1 part manure and 1 part leafmould

Of course, you can improvise upon the above and make your own amendments – depending on what materials you have, and what consistency you are looking for. I find coarse sand or fine grit (available at garden centres) a useful ingredient. It helps with drainage, so that the mix never becomes waterlogged, but it also helps to retain water in dry conditions, as each grain of sand attracts a film of moisture to itself.

THE GARDEN YEAR

'Time is what prevents everything from happening at once.'
John Archibald Wheeler, theoretical physicist

WINTER

Winter is the lean and chill time of the year: leaner and chiller for some than for others, depending on your whereabouts. Our own garden is a third of a mile (0.5 kilometres) from the sea – as the seagull flies – so most years frost is rare and snow is almost non-existent. There is no well-defined transition between the seasons in this mild part of this mild island. Our seasons slide slyly into each other, rather than jolting rudely from one to the next, as they do in more extreme climates. On some days, winter seems more like a lack of light and an absence of activity than anything more dramatic.

Yet these sombre days are an important part of the yearly cycle of life. They mark the lowest and slowest part of the rotation of nature's ever-revolving wheel – the quiet near-pause before it spins upwards again into growth. Most plants are dormant; the life has drained out of them, leaving only sere remains or collapsed, sodden material. Annuals and second-year biennials have all but finished their life's work; a few bits of seed remain, but most has been shed or dispersed, and the next generation is already taking its chances in the soil. With perennials, and biennials that have yet to flower, the vitality has flowed back underground and locked itself up in roots and rhizomes, bulbs and corms.

A few trees, shrubs and perennials are evergreen, and are quietly ticking over, doing the minimum to stay alive. These bolster up the structure of the winter garden, giving the eye somewhere green to rest for a moment. They also provide a place of shelter for birds and overwintering invertebrates. Tiny platoons of aphids may be found bivouacking amongst the leaves, but don't be tempted to send them to their maker. Instead, let the sparrows and other small birds clear them out; they need protein-rich meals such as these during this meagre period.

Plants other than evergreens also retain a striking presence in the garden: trees with naked branches make dark silhouettes in the low light, and certain herbaceous plants, although quite dead, leave elegant skeletons standing like gaunt effigies of their former selves. The lifeless, bony frameworks of perennials, annuals and biennials are best after sunny summers and autumns, when the warmth hardens and dries out the remains. Damp and mild weather

A chestnut tree in a nearby park creates a noble silhouette in the fog of a winter's morning.

A blue tit stocks up on bird cake on a snowy winter day: high energy food such as this helps small birds to stay alive in cold weather.

leaves the autumn garden in collapse, but even in a soggy year, some species always make fine upstanding corpses. When touched by frost, and backlit by the low, almost monochromatic light of winter, a crisply dead plant has all the drama of a black-and-white etching. When you're deciding what to plant in a garden, be sure to include some plants that look beautiful in mortal repose.

I have a soft spot for the aptly named Miss Willmott's ghost (*Eryngium giganteum*) – a biennial sea holly from the Caucusus and Iran, and so called because the British gardener Ellen Willmott (1858–1934) was said to have surreptitiously dropped its seed around gardens that she toured, as a delayed reminder of her visit. When alive, her namesake is a light-reflecting silver with frosty pewter flowers, beloved of bees. It fades to an interesting pale beige in death, beautifully taut and spiny.

Teasel, another biennial, is one of the best plant skeletons, being both sculptural and long lasting. Its oval, spiky seed heads and tall bristly stem give it a fierce, warrior-like presence in the winter garden. The seeds, hidden deep between aggressive barbs, attract goldfinches, which winkle them out patiently with their precise bills. These little birds often travel in small groups, and are everyone's favourites, wearing neat buff-and-white suits jazzily decorated with red, black and yellow.

Birds bring life to the winter garden when most of the plants are sleeping. Their antics and acrobatics are entertaining for us, yet for them, this busy foraging and eating is the only way to stay alive during the short, cold days. In the dark months of December and January, small birds such as wrens and blue tits can easily lose 10 per cent of their body weight just keeping warm

The spiny remains of Miss Willmott's ghost (*Eryngium giganteum*) wearing a shiny cap of melting snow; and frost decorating the serrated leaves and pink-flushed flowers of *Helleborus* x *sternii*

during the long nights. (I know I mentioned this earlier, but the figure is so dramatic, I feel it's worth repeating.) They need to start eating first thing in the morning and keep at it all day: it's a full-time job. Obviously, they'll do better in a garden with lots of seed heads and berries, and – if you are so minded – extra food on the bird table, in hanging feeders and scattered on the ground. Don't forget to check that their source of water isn't frozen on icy mornings.

A FEW BRAVE PLANTS

Although some plants are quietly developing their roots underground, at soil level much of the garden is slumbering. Yet in the midst of this stillness there are a few hardy souls flowering, lifting our spirits with their blooms. Winter flowers are so few that each one is a cause for celebration. Many are borne close to the ground: among them the lovely, washed-out mauve Algerian iris (*I. unguicularis*) and its tiny Turkish cousin, the canary-yellow *I. danfordiae*. This is also the season for hellebores, which starts with the appropriately named, creamy-flowered Christmas rose (*Helleborus niger*). Following close on its heels are the Corsican hellebore (*H. argutifolius*), the unfairly tagged stinking hellebore (*H. foetidus*) and the terribly chic Oriental hybrids. Snowdrops appear on the cusp of spring.

Most shrubs and trees have withdrawn into dormancy, but a few, such as winter-flowering cherry, witch hazels and daphnes, have unbuttoned their buds to produce welcome flowers (these last two are highly perfumed). Others step forward into the picture with interesting bark and stem. Aside from these rare performers, it is a time of quietude among the plants, as they conserve their energy for the spring surge.

This witch hazel *Hamamelis* x *intermedia* 'Diane' has little fragrance, but its deep rusty-red flowers add a richness that is welcome in winter.

WINTER WARMERS: SHRUBS AND TREES FOR WINTER INTEREST
Winter blossom
- Daphne, including *D. bholua* 'Jacqueline Postill': evergreen shrub, highly scented pink flowers (which attract winter bumblebees); *D.b.* 'Gurkha', similar, but deciduous and hardier; *D. odora*, evergreen shrub with pinky-purple flowers
- Witch hazel (*Hamamelis* spp.): deciduous shrubs, including the yellow *H.* × *intermedia* 'Pallida', which is reputed to be the most scented; rusty and ruby-flowered cultivars such as 'Jelena' and 'Diane' have little fragrance, but are an unusual colour for this time of the year; best in moist soil
- Winter jasmine (*Jasminum nudiflorum*), deciduous shrub with yellow flowers on dark green stems; grow against a wall and prune immediately after flowering
- Winter-flowering cherry (*Prunus* × *subhirtella* 'Autumnalis'): deciduous tree, shell-pink flowers appear intermittently from November to April
- *Viburnum* × *bodnantense* 'Dawn': deciduous, upright shrub with pink, scented flowers from autumn to spring; easy to grow
- Also winter sweet (*Chimonanthes praecox*), Persian ironwood (*Parrotia persica*), *Mahonia* spp., *Sarcococca* spp.

Winter-flowering cherry, *Prunus* x *subhirtella* 'Autumnalis', blooms intermittently for the six coldest months of the year. It provides nectar for winter-foraging bumblebees.

Winter bark and stems

Barking trees:
- Paperbark maple (*Acer griseum*): peeling, rust-coloured bark; extremely slow growing
- Birch: the whitest is *Betula utilis* var. *jacquemontii*
- *Prunus serrula*: shiny, copper-brown trunk and limbs
- Also snakebark maples: *A. capillipes*, *A. davidii*, *A. pensylvanicum* and *A. rufinerve*

Show-stopping stems:
- Dogwood (*Cornus* spp.): *C. alba* 'Sibirica' has bright crimson stems while 'Elegantissima' is maroon with variegated leaves; *C. sanguinea* 'Midwinter Fire' has orange and red stems; *C. sericea* 'Flavirimea' has olive-green; dogwoods grown for winter colour should be pruned back to the base in spring (around March) every year or two
- Ghost brambles (*Rubus* spp.): well named, with purplish stems overlaid with a sepulchral pale bloom; prickly and vigorous *R. cockburnianus* is only for large gardens; *R. thibetanus* is better behaved, but must still be closely monitored; prune as for dogwood
- Willow (*Salix* spp.): *S. alba* var. *vitellina* has egg-yolk yellow stems, while those of its cultivar 'Britzensis' are scarlet; *S. daphnoides* has purple shoots dusted with a white bloom; prune as for dogwood; be sure to save the stems for lightweight plant supports or for weaving

The pretty annual love-in-a-mist (*Nigella damascena*), and the biennial teasel (*Dipsacus* sp.) have fine winter skeletons; goldfinches are partial to the seeds of *Dipsacus*.

LOVELY SKELETONS: PLANTS THAT LOOK GOOD DEAD
Many of these will also supply seeds for the birds
- Perennials: *Acanthus spinosus*, *Agapanthus*, artichoke (*Cynara scolymus*), *Astilbe*, *Echinacea*, *Eryngium*, *Eupatorium*, *Inula magnifica*, many iris (including *I. foetidissima*, *I. pseudacorus* and *I. sibirica*), *Phlomis russeliana*, *Rudbeckia*, large *Sedum* species and cultivars.
- Annuals and biennials: foxglove (*Digitalis*), love-in-a-mist (*Nigella*), Miss Willmott's ghost (*Eryngium giganteum*), mullein (*Verbascum*), Scotch thistle (*Onopordum acanthium*), shoo-fly (*Nicandra physalodes*), sunflower (*Helianthus annuus*), teasel (*Dipsacus fullonum*).
- Some grasses, including *Calamagrostis brachytricha*, *Deschampsia cespitosa*, *Miscanthus*, *Stipa*.

WINTER WORK
I don't believe in annual digging as a general prescription for vegetable gardens. But many gardeners disagree with me. This is the time when they are out spading the soil, leaving it in rough clods and letting the expanding and contracting action of freezing and melting further shatter the structure. Good luck to them and their backs.

However, now is a good time to dig trenches for hedges and holes for trees (providing that the ground is not waterlogged or frozen), and to plant during mild spells. If you need to move young trees and shrubs, it can be done now, while they are dormant. Otherwise, stay off the soil as much as possible, as the damp and relatively inactive earth is easily compacted.

If you bought bulbs in autumn and forgot about them, don't panic: they can be planted right up to the end of the year, and even later (better to gamble with them in the ground than discard them on to the compost heap).

Look out for the emerging shoots of snowdrops and daffodils and clear any dead perennials around them so that they can get light and air.

If you grow hellebores, take a critical look at them: if the lower leaves are tired and mottled with black (the latter from a common fungal disease, hellebore leaf blotch, *Coniothyrium hellebori*), remove them now. New, unblemished leaves will quickly grow back.

Try to keep the garden picture from tipping from a dignified and skeletal tableau into a mouldering mess. As plants collapse, cut them back. Compost them, or roughly chop and tuck under shrubs, where you won't notice them. There they will decay naturally, attracting creepy-crawlies and worms – and ground-foraging birds such as blackbirds and dunnocks.

Beware of wind-rock: where plants become loosened by being constantly blown about. Overwintering brassicas, such as Brussels sprouts and sprouting broccoli are susceptible. Earth up the stems or secure them with stakes or plant hoops. Rose bushes are also vulnerable: a light pruning (reducing them by about half or a third) will give the wind less purchase. Their final pruning will be in spring, so this can be fast and rough.

In the vegetable garden, garlic can be planted, and broad beans can be sown from late winter into early spring. (You can sow broad beans from late autumn, but only if your soil is well drained – and even then the seeds may rot before they germinate.)

If snow falls, keep essential paths and steps clear by sweeping or shovelling. Heavy snow should be gently knocked off hedges and shrubs if it is in danger of damaging them. A sprinkling of wood ash will make icy paths less slippery and is much kinder to plants than salt.

A patch of winter garden where *Phlomis russeliana* and *Calamagrostis* grasses show off their good bones.

Now – while the garden is at its most sparse, and before the spring rush – is the season to undertake painting, repairs and construction work.

Take some time to take stock of the year that has just passed. Make notes about what might be changed, and where you hit the bull's eye. Believe me, such records will be useful – if only to amuse you – in the coming years. Decide what you are going to grow, and order seed catalogues or make use of online catalogues.

Winter is the only period where we get a breather from the garden – which makes it the natural time for planning and reflecting.

SPRING

Spring is the most exciting time in the garden. Some years, it starts almost imperceptibly, with a few shy bulbs poking out of the soil like the nose cones of miniature green rockets, waiting to blast into flower. And on trees and shrubs, buds swell, poised to break open and reveal packages of fresh leaves. Other years, the season arrives all in a rush, and the throb of growth and renewal is palpable.

With bulbs, this swell of energy has been building invisibly since autumn: below ground, the basal plate has pushed a few careful roots into the soil and the inner tissues have been quietly

Narcissus, scilla and anemones naturalized on the banks of the Vartry River at Mount Usher, Co. Wicklow.

transforming into embryonic shoots and flower stems. By the time spring arrives, an entire plant-in-waiting – roots, shoots, leaves and flower – has been assembled in the core of the bulb. As the days lengthen, a pale and waxy hatchling emerges, surging upwards through the soil and turning green when it nudges into the light. Bulbs are always dramatic, as the blooms arrive speedily and fully formed, unlike those of herbaceous or woody plants, for which there is often an agonizing wait while they muster enough supportive green material before they can think about flowering.

The season gives us crocuses, snowdrops, scilla, daffodils, bluebells, tulips and other bulbous plants. It is also the time for the perennial woodlanders, plants that in their natural habitat live under deciduous trees, where they flower early, before the canopy of leaves dims the light. Alpine plants are in bloom also. These are the showy little gems, such as gentians and pasque flowers (*Pulsatilla*), that grow on mountainsides in the wild, and in the rockeries and scree beds of plant fanatics.

Spring-flowering shrubs and trees begin to blossom too, with more abandon than the species that cautiously perform in winter. In the landscape, luminous gorse and blackthorn herald the new season: the first cheerfully golden and the second frothily white. They line the roads and motorways in Ireland, making me wish that my garden were large enough to have a wild perimeter of these optimistically flowered plants.

The weather in spring is changeable. These mercurial months offer bitter cold and frost, blustery wind and rain, balmy sunshine and growth-provoking warmth – sometimes in quick

Precious spring blooms: the Turkish snowdrop (*Galanthus elwesii*) and a pasque flower (*Pulsatilla* sp.).

succession, and in no fixed order. The conditions may leap backwards into winter overnight, which explains the Irish proverb: 'April borrowed three days of March to kill the old cow.'

Regardless of cow-killing freezes, the days become brighter, and soon there is 'a grand stretch in the evenings' – and in the mornings too. Which is just as well, as this is a busy time for wildlife. All the garden's creatures have their minds on procreation. Frogs appear in ponds, the females heavy with eggs, the males charged with sperm and hormones. Their mating procedure, called amplexus, results in mounds of spawn. In many ponds the wobbly islands of jelly-insulated eggs arrive at the same time each year: in ours it's usually within a day or two of Valentine's Day, 14 February. Snails and slugs, although they may have been active on warmer winter days, are more in evidence now. They also have *l'amour* on their minds, and may be found on mild, damp days tied into ecstatic knots. Dinner is likewise on their agenda. At this time of the year they can inflict grievous damage on emerging foliage by chomping through layers of still furled leaves. Seedlings may also be polished off overnight if precautions are not taken.

Meanwhile, the birds are preoccupied with claiming territories, and – in the case of the males – making a huge hoo-ha about what-a-great-bird-am-I. The shenanigans are mighty: strutting, dancing, fluffing, puffing, bouncing, fly-diving and all manner of showing off. Hen birds select their mates (or in the case of dunnocks, they may indulge in a spot of polygamy). Nest building and egg laying gets under way, with long working hours, from first to last light. This is the time for gardeners to avoid disturbing nest places (such as hedges and other dense

A gang of mating frogs in our tiny pond; the swollen belly of the female can be seen at the bottom of the bundle.

woody growth), and perhaps to leave useful bits of building material around. In our garden, we put hair from the dog brush on the bird table, from where it is carried off for insulation. (I like to think of a brood of blue tits cosied up in a nest lined with Milo's and Lily's warm fur.)

Spring sees the first explosion of aphids. In our garden they materialize on rose buds and tulips, and on the two evergreen spurges with the impossible names *Euphorbia characias* subsp. *wulfenii* and *E. amygdaloides* var. *robbiae* (in America the latter goes by the sensible and more pleasing appellation Mrs Robb's bonnet). Sparrows, greenfinches and tits go mad for the huddles of little green insects, and the euphorbia clumps shimmy with the busy rummagings of the birds. Early aphids are an important food crop, not just for the birds but for the larvae of ladybirds, hoverflies and lacewings.

Butterflies come flitting into the open in spring: raggedy small tortoiseshells and peacocks that have overwintered in a tree crevice or shed; and freshly minted orange tips, holly blues and speckled woods that have just emerged from their pupae. Honeybees return to work, foraging for nectar and pollen among the euphorbias, as well as other early bloomers such as anemone, aubrieta, bergenia, bluebell, crocus and dandelion.

Spring is harvest time for my favourite vegetable, purple sprouting broccoli. It's nutty-tasting and tender, and leaping with vitamins and iron. I look forward to the first blue-flushed florets of the year with the barely containable excitement of a wine buff anticipating *le premier verre* of Beaujolais Nouveau.

A blue tit drops by to collect some dog hair to line its nest, while a sparrow cleans early aphids from a euphorbia plant.

Spring bulbs: *Narcissus* 'Actaea' and *Fritillaria meleagris*; both are suitable for naturalizing in grass.

A FEW BULBOUS CHARACTERS (INCLUDING CORMS, RHIZOMES AND TUBERS)

Snowdrop (*Galanthus*), snowflake (*Leucojum vernum*), crocus, cyclamen, scilla, daffodil (*Narcissus*), bluebell (native *Hyacinthoides non-scripta* and its Spanish cousin, *H. hispanica*), tulip (*Tulipa*), anemone (including *A. blanda*, *A. nemorosa* and *A. apennina*), grape hyacinth (*Muscari*), glory of the snow (*Chionodoxa*), *Fritillaria*.

FIRST-PAST-THE-POST PERENNIALS

There are dozens of desirable early perennials, but we would be all day listing each and every one of them. Instead, here are just a few to be going on with: lungwort (*Pulmonaria*), bergenia (also known as elephant's ears), erythronium, epimedium, Solomon's seal (*Polygonatum* × *hybridum*), primroses and all kinds of *Primula*, and spurges (*Euphorbia*) aplenty.

SOME WOODY SPRING THINGS

If you are lucky enough to have humus-rich soil and a large garden, camellias, magnolias and rhododendrons are yours to grow. Rhodos and camellias require lots of calming green to offset their big, noisy flowers, and look out of place in a smaller garden. (Don't even consider planting or doing anything nice to *Rhododendron ponticum*, the mauve-flowered beast that has naturalized in parts of Ireland and Britain. It is a plant pest of the highest order, smothering our native flora and turning parts of these islands into a monocultural rhododendron wasteland.) The flowering dogwoods (*Cornus*) also like a lime-free, fertile soil. The *Viburnum* genus is more adaptable: most of these shrubs and small trees are equally at home in acid to slightly alkaline soil. Both the wayfaring tree (*V. lantana*) and the guelder rose (*V. opulus*) are happiest in very alkaline soil.

Spring also gives us blossom on the *Rosaceae* clan: the apples (*Malus* – both domestic and crab), hawthorn (*Crataegus*), rowan (*Sorbus*), juneberry (*Amelanchier*) and, of course, the cherries (*Prunus*). All are beloved of bees when in flower, and of birds when in berry.

Clematis are getting into their upward stride. Those flowering now include the evergreen *C. armandii* (the cultivar 'Apple Blossom' has bigger blooms than the species) and all the many manifestations of *C. montana*.

SPRING WORK

The warming soil is undiscriminating as to whether it propels the growth of weeds or of cherished plants and seedlings. But weeds that germinate on fallow ground do no harm (as long as you are draconian about pulling them before they seed). On the contrary, they help protect the structure of the soil and keep it active. They will compete with emerging plants, however, and newly planted hedges, shrubs and trees, so do keep the soil around these weed free. When you have cleared, apply a mulch to protect the soil surface, preferably after a heavy spring rain. If the season is dry, then give a really good watering before you mulch: this is well-spent water, helping the roots to make a strong framework that will be better able to gather moisture later, and to act as an anchor.

Perennial weeds, such as bindweed and dandelion, are another matter: keep on top of these as soon as they appear. But keep a clump or two of nettles. Small tortoiseshell, peacock and red admiral butterflies lay their eggs exclusively on nettles, which then become the food plants for their caterpillars.

Snowdrops and other early bulbs can be lifted and divided after they finish flowering, but while they are still 'in the green'. Do this only if they are too crowded, have become shy of flowering or are required elsewhere.

Now is the busiest time of the year for seed sowing and potting on. If you have a polytunnel or greenhouse, you can sow leaves (lettuce, spinach, rocket, et al.), and in just a few weeks you'll have fresh green things for the salad bowl. These can be replaced in a couple of months by tomatoes and other tender crops.

Seeds may be sown outside also, in the ground (if you are confident that you can ward off slugs and snails) and in trays or modules. Warm-season crops such as tomatoes, aubergines, peppers, courgettes and beans can be sown indoors with heat (on a sunny windowsill or in a propagator). Remember, however, that they can't go outdoors until there is no risk of frost, and until then, they need good, bright light if they are not to become etiolated (a word I was taught in biology class when I was eleven, and which I like to use as much as possible: it means pale and drawn, because of lack of light). Therefore, unless you have a greenhouse or sunny conservatory, delay sowing these tender crops until late spring.

Potatoes should go into the ground around mid-spring: some people like to plant them on St Patrick's Day, others wait until Good Friday – even though the date of the latter moveable feast may vary by as much as four weeks. But never mind that; the important thing is to get them planted sometime around now.

If you didn't do so in autumn, sow nectar-rich annuals, including poached-egg plant (*Limnanthes douglasii*), cornflower (*Centaurea cyanus*), pot marigold (*Calendula officinalis*) and love-in-a-mist (*Nigella damascena*).

Prune roses in early spring, and give them a mulch of something nutritious. Dogwoods, willows and ghost brambles that are grown for their colourful winter stems should be cut back to near the base. If you grow buddlejas for your butterflies, the stems can be shortened to about a third of their length. (When pruning anything, always remove all the dead and dodgy-looking growth first.)

Purple sprouting broccoli is in full production now. Harvest the main cluster of florets at the top of the plant first, and continue to pick from the sides as soon as the buds are large enough. Big, healthy plants will crop for a good six weeks.

Cast a quick eye over the garden pond. Clear away dead growth, and if there is too much vegetation or algae, haul some of it out now – but not if you have tadpoles, as they tend to get mixed up in the greenery. (Frogspawn takes ten days to four weeks to hatch, so you can work gingerly around it just after it has appeared.)

Finally, make an effort to get out of your garden and into someone else's. Spring is a magical time, and is sometimes best enjoyed when we're not thinking of the next pressing task. Gardens in Ireland that charm me in this season are Mount Usher, Kilmacurragh and Annes Grove.

SUMMER

Summer sunshine and heat are never a sure thing out here on the edge of Europe. The temperature on a cloudy afternoon in June might be the same as that on a balmy December day – hovering around 12°C (54°F). But there is a world of difference in the quality and quantity of light. The day of the winter solstice gives us only seven and a half hours of milky illumination, as the sun skims low in our northern European sky, before returning to its summer duties on the other side of the globe. Yet our mid-summer sun overwhelms us with attention, bathing us in a full seventeen hours of daylight. After dusk, it slips away only a few degrees over the horizon, from where it gives the night sky a reassuring glow.

Even if there are clouds and rain – as there often are – the long, long days that leak into the brief nights mean that this can only be summer. The early part of the season is green and fresh: foliage is still young and unblemished, and many flowering plants are in their first enthusiastic flush. Most pests and diseases have yet to muster their forces (except for aphids and molluscs, of course, which have been out and about – and busy enough – since spring). There is a manageability about the garden; plants maintain some decorum and neatness. Even the fancy-pants oriental poppies and the flashily spiked lupins are relatively polite about not encroaching on their neighbours. Yet within weeks the garden has expanded into a bustling, overflowing, ungovernable mass of vegetation. Plants grow taller and wider, hiding the earth beneath them and covering surfaces around them with climbing and scrambling stems. There is a free-for-all in the borders and beds, and flowering and fruiting in plenty. In the vegetable garden produce is coming off the plants and out of the ground faster than we can eat it, preserve it, pickle it, freeze it or dry it.

It is a far cry from the austere days of winter, when one's entire attention is captured by a few green shoots and brave blooms. By late summer, there is an almost unbearable abundance of vegetation and a kind of botanical hecticity. Each plant, hurtling towards autumn, is in a self-serving frenzy to flower, get pollinated and make seed before the seasonal change leaches the energy from its tissues.

For the bird population, the frantic phase is during the earlier half of summer. Quiet and secretive days of egg brooding come to an abrupt end when the shells are cudgelled open from within. Each chick, using an egg tooth – a temporary protrusion on the upper part of the bill – cracks out into the world. Before long, with its mouth stretched as wide as its head, the nestling is straining for food. The brightly coloured funnel formed by the insistently craning throat is impossible for the parents to ignore. It demands to be filled with protein – flies, aphids, grubs, worms. The adult birds must hunt for long hours feeding the squealing, gobbling apparatus that is attached to their helpless offspring. Their job is easier in a garden where insecticides have not been used, and it's safer too: I once witnessed a family of tits being wiped out after they had eaten insects that had been poisoned by a pest controller.

Young birds grow fast, and leave the nest within two weeks, even though they may not be able

High summer in June Blake's Garden, Co. Wicklow, with dahlias, crocosmia, red hot pokers and lilies in full song.

Dragonflies spend up to four years underwater as larvae, but their days in the air are limited to just a few weeks.

to fly for another couple of days. Although these flightless fledglings may look abandoned and pathetic, there is usually no call for alarm, as their parents are not far off. While waiting for muscles and wing feathers to develop, the new generation is vulnerable to attack from other birds and from cats. You can't do much about the former, but if you are a cat owner, do try to restrict your pet's garden time in early summer.

After the baby-filled days during the first part of the season, the birds settle down to a quieter existence. The adults have done their jobs producing and rearing their progeny, and have no further parental responsibilities. Territorial battles and mating games are suspended for the moment. For some, it is a time to retire to the shelter of shrubs and hedges for the yearly moult. The shedding of old, worn-out feathers and their replacement with thick, new ones dresses their owners appropriately for the coming winter.

Swifts, which are among the last of our migrants to arrive in May, are the quintessential summer birds, especially for those of us in urban areas. Their black boomerang wings and forked fuselages glide high and dip low in the sky, and their screeching calls pierce the air. They never land on the ground, but carry out all their life's activities on the wing, except for nesting and rearing young – often in the eaves of old houses. But in August, they are the first to go, returning to Africa and leaving behind an empty sky.

Butterflies are more in evidence during the latter half of the summer. Peacocks, painted ladies and red admirals – which have been rare earlier in the season – erupt from their pupae hidden in the long grass, nettles and thistles in the wilder parts of the garden. They sun themselves on warm walls and stonework before fluttering off to feed on nectar-rich flowers. Some will attempt to migrate south, others to hibernate, while others will perish before the year is over. Their lives are short but showy.

In the garden pond, damselflies and dragonflies emerge from late spring and into summer. They have spent the first two to four years of their lives underwater as fearsome, carnivorous nymphs. Their glory days in the sun are scant in comparison. After shrugging off their nymphal skins, they hunt on the air, mate (sometimes while airborne) and lay eggs in the water. And after a few weeks, they die.

The tadpoles that hatched in the pond in late spring have a longer adult life ahead of them. By now they are miniature frogs, flawless likenesses of their parents. It will take nearly

Spires of foxgloves and the open dishes of hardy geraniums (such as 'Rozanne') populate the summer garden.

another two years before they are sexually mature, but they can look forward to a lifespan of seven or eight years.

SUMMER FLOWERS

There are hundreds of good plants that flower during this profligate time, and it would take a whole book to write about them. (As it happens, I can recommend that very item for the latter half of the season, in Marina Christopher's *Late Summer Flowers*.) But we have room to consider only a few here, so I'll stick to a handful that perform over a long period, or that are so spectacular that we forgive them their fleeting appearance.

In the here-today-gone-tomorrow category are the herbaceous peonies. Some flower in late spring, but the thousands of cultivars of *P. lactiflora*, which include old-fashioned cottage favourites, bloom from June onwards. The scented, flamboyant petals are floored by wind or rain, but for the week or two that they are with us, they are the glitterati of the garden. Around the same time, we have the dizzying spires of biennial foxgloves (*Digitalis purpurea*), and the cartoonish, bouncing balls of the *Allium* tribe (for late summer there is the smaller, elongated *A. sphaerocephalon*). Hardy geraniums swarm all over the garden in summer; newer cultivars such as 'Rozanne' and 'Brookside' go on well into autumn if you deadhead them regularly. These bright days also belong to the South Africans: the strings-of-stars crocosmias, the celestial fishing rods of the *Dierama* and the first fiery pokers of the *Kniphofia* tribe.

The American perennial daisies are also out in force, filling the middle air with petalled flying saucers and crazy summer hats. Among them are the coneflowers (*Rudbeckia* and *Echinacea*), tickseed (*Helenium*), sunflowers (*Helianthus*), oxeye (*Heliopsis*) and rosinweed (*Silphium*). Goldenrod (*Solidago*) and Joe Pye weed (*Eupatorium*) are members of the same family that are also in bloom now – although their appearance belies their affiliations. All are in great demand by nectar-sipping insects.

Summer also gives us affable annual flowers in meadows, beds and borders; haughty lilies that patronize us with their majestic trumpets; and elegant grasses with inflorescences that shine silver and gold against the dawn and evening light.

This is the time of year when those most historic and sumptuous of shrubs, the roses, are in flower. Another woody plant that rivals them for scent is the mock orange (*Philadelphus*): the French-bred 'Belle Étoile' is one of the sweetest. *Buddleja davidii* lives up to its common name, the butterfly bush, and is mobbed by eager lepidopterans. Fuchsias flower all summer, jingling their pink and purple bells in the breeze. The faux petals of hydrangeas are beginning to change colour, and not for the last time before they finally call it a day at the end of autumn. Honeysuckle and clematis are going up and around and through the garden. If you have trouble growing the latter, look for those with *Clematis viticella* in their parentage, as they are vigorous and resistant to wilt – the disease that can fell a full-grown plant in days. Among those that are often found in garden centres are 'Étoile Violette', 'Kermesina' and 'Polish Spirit'.

SUMMER WORK

Every plant's ultimate aim in life is to produce seeds, to secure the future of its species. So when you grow plants for the pleasure of their flowers, you must discourage them from setting seed and 'thinking' that their year's work is done. Regular deadheading (removing the spent blooms) keeps their energies focused on flower production. However, some plants – such as *Phlomis* and ornamental grasses – produce architectural seed heads that are pleasing to both gardeners and birds, so leave them be.

Lady's mantle (*Alchemilla mollis*) should be deadheaded after flowering to prevent it leaving its babies all over the place. You can shear back the foliage while you're at it, to promote a fresh crop of leaves. This approach can be used also for ground-covering hardy geraniums that flower in late spring and early summer, if their leaves are looking weary. Strawberries that have finished fruiting will also benefit from a haircut.

Prune philadelphus, deutzia and weigela after flowering; and if you need to do formative pruning (that is, shaping while young) on members of the cherry clan (*Prunus*), do it now. Take stem-tip cuttings of penstemons, fuchsia, tender geraniums (*Pelargonium*) and other tender or borderline summer lovelies.

If you grow water lilies in your garden pond, remove the old flowers and dead leaves, so that they don't sink to the bottom and rot. Keep an eye out for blanket weed – mats of pale green algae formed of tiny filaments – and remove it. You may need to thin out some of the oxygenating plants in the water as well, if it is too crowded. But do be careful of tadpoles and froglets. Leave all this green detritus by the side of the water overnight so that the creatures in it have a chance to make their way back home.

Sow purple sprouting broccoli and kale in early summer, and transplant the young plants to their final positions in the garden in July or August. Sow salad crops every few weeks during the summer, so that there is a steady flow of leaves for months, instead of a fortnight-long deluge of lettuces.

Keep weeding, weeding and weeding in the tamer parts of the garden, to prevent unwanted invaders from interfering with your other plants. But do look for self-sown seedlings of desirable garden plants while you are on your hands and knees wrestling dandelions.

Finally, some important advice: although the garden is clamouring for attention all summer long, do take time to sit quietly now and again. Within half an hour, birds, frogs and other creatures get used to the human in their garden, and they carry on their most interesting lives, oblivious to the interloper in their midst.

A summer border in June Blake's garden, with persicaria, rudbeckia, thalictrum, phlox and other perennials.

In late October, plants take on warm autumnal hues in the Dillon Garden in Dublin.

AUTUMN

Autumn is a season of two personalities, as it careers wildly between summery cheerfulness and end-of-year cold and gloom. At times, there are magic hours when the synergy between the two moods is absolute, with glowing light, crisp air and good smells. The perfect autumn day is bathed in golden-syrup luminescence and perfumed like the inside of a pumpkin: sharp, vegetal and ripe. Such days are precious, as they are painted on a canvas of dwindling light and waning energy. Beneath the splendour of autumn there is a stillness that is not far from death. Winter is waiting around the corner.

But before that season catches hold, some plants still have important work to do, ensuring a future for their progeny. Seed must be ripened and then dispersed – by wind, animals or self-propulsion. Some of this seed is embedded in lustrous fruits, in every shade from white to black, and in all the colours of the spectrum in between. Red berries are the favourite of birds: they dine on the flesh, and some time after their meal, they deposit the intact seed in a new location. Because it always attracts diners, nature chooses red more often than any other colour for berries. Ruby-coloured fruits please human eyes too, and add a festive note to the autumn garden.

Some plants are only now flowering, in a last hurrah before retirement. September and

October (and November, in milder areas) give us dahlias, asters, sedums, ornamental grasses and other late bloomers. Bright colours that can be brash and blinding in the high light of summer become full bodied and sonorous in the low rays of autumn.

The greatest feat of nature during this season is that of the changing of the leaves, where the trees swap their calm green mantle for a blazing patchwork of gold, orange and crimson. Strangely, the yellow and orange pigments (xanthophylls and carotenoids respectively) are already present in the leaf, hidden under the green layer, like a set of peachy underclothes. They are revealed only at the end of the growing season, when the chlorophyll breaks down, having completed its work of photosynthesis. No matter what the weather, golden tones appear on autumn foliage.

The scarlets, carmines and purples are another matter. These pigments, called anthocyanins, are manufactured by excess sugars in the leaves. Bright autumn days and cold (but not freezing) nights create the most vibrant displays. During the daytime the sun helps create the anthocyanins, while at night the low temperatures gradually seal off the veins, so that the pigments are unable to leak away. At this quietening time of the year, the oblique light seems to set these leaves on fire, so that each autumn-ignited tree and shrub stands out like a beacon.

The webs of garden spiders glisten in the morning dew. They are woven anew overnight by their owners, beefy individuals with geometric white markings on their tubby abdomens and a dizzying number of jazzily striped legs. Before spinning a new web, they have a midnight feast of the old one, and whatever insects have become ensnared in it. At this time of the year the males – half the size of the formidable females – make overtures to their potential partners. This is a dangerous business and can go horribly wrong, with suitor ending up as supper rather than spouse. After mating, the spider bride lays scores of eggs, encased in a silken sac. Exhausted from the effort, she perishes, but her spiderlings, miniature replicas of their mother, appear in spring.

Butterflies are active in autumn, and while a few species overwinter as larvae or eggs, and a few as adults, most do not survive.

Swallows and other migrant birds are much in evidence, noisily feeding up for the long journey ahead. We don't have swallows in our town garden, but country friends tell me that they feel bereft when their flocks suddenly depart in September, leaving a hush behind them. (Other friends are relieved that the chore of cleaning the streaks of droppings off their barn doors is finished until spring.) As one species leaves, another appears. Migrant thrushes, such as fieldfares and redwings, arrive. These join our native thrushes and blackbirds to eat autumn berries, to drill our lawns for leatherjackets and other grubs and to gorge on windfalls under apple trees.

Smaller birds such as sparrows and other finches, robins, tits and warblers feed on autumn's bounty, preparing for the winter ahead. Now that nesting, mating and chick rearing is over, they are less frenetic and less territorial.

As the season shifts towards colder days and longer nights, outdoor mice come indoors, and long-limbed, athletic house spiders start wandering around looking for mates. Both of these skittery happenings test my devotion to wildlife, but are proof that nature does not stop at the back door – particularly in autumn.

The wine-stained plumes of *Miscanthus* 'Malepartus', animated in the autumn breeze. The mopheads of this hydrangea are suffused with red.

AUTUMN BLOOMERS: FLOWERING PLANTS THAT ARE GOOD FOR A LAST BLAST
Perennials

The following provide nectar for butterflies and bees: *Aster* cvs (*A. amellus* 'King George', *A. × frikartii* 'Mönch' and *A.* 'Little Carlow' are good purples, *A. novae-angliae* 'Andenken an Alma Pötsche' is bright pink, while *A. divaricatus*, the white wood aster, is happy in a shady area); *Dahlia* cultivars, until hit by frost; Joe Pye weed (*Eupatorium purpureum*) needs some moisture; *Gaura lindheimeri*, dry soil; perennial sunflower cultivars (*Helianthus*); *Salvia* – some are a little tender; large *Sedum* species and cultivars. Hardy geraniums that received a post-flowering haircut in summer are now showing a second flush. Less attractive to insects, but providing late colour and invaluable for dry shade are the Japanese anemones and the diminutive lily turf (*Liriope muscari*). Red hot pokers (*Kniphofia*) – which may equally be orange or lemon – are fine, rousing autumn plants, especially if planted en masse; they require sunshine and some moisture. If you have a shady spot and humusy soil, the toad lilies (*Tricyrtis*) will offer up their spotted, sea-creature blooms.

Grasses

Miscanthus (many cultivars) have tasselled inflorescences in silver, grey and wine; the switch grasses (*Panicum*) have fine beadlike flower heads, borne on wiry stems; and the flowers of *Pennisetum alopecuroides* are like those big bristly caterpillars known as 'hairy mollies' in Ireland.

Bulbous blooms

The so-called autumn crocus (*Colchicum*), which is actually a member of the lily family; the true autumn crocus (*Crocus speciosus*) and saffron crocus (*C. sativum*); *Cyclamen hederifolium*; *Schizostylis coccinea* (moist soil, full sun) has bright crimson flowers, but there are several cultivars, ranging from white and peach to pink. The South African *Nerine bowdenii* and *Amaryllis belladonna* are for mild gardens, or need a warm and sheltered position.

Flowering shrubs

Caryopteris, smallish, silvery-leaved shrub with clear blue flowers; hardy plumbago (*Ceratostigma*), low, ground-cover shrub with brilliant blue flowers and leaves that turn red and wine in autumn (needs warm position); incense bush (*Ageratina ligustrina*), medium-sized, evergreen with frothy white flowers, beloved of butterflies (warm position and well-drained soil); *Hydrangea* (many cultivars): the flowers of some of the blowsy mophead types (*H. macrophylla*) turn chintzy shades of deep red in autumn.

BERRIES

The rose family (*Rosaceae*) is blessed with superb berriers – all of which are attractive to birds. The *Sorbus* genus (rowans and whitebeams, many of which also have vibrant autumn foliage) is probably the most popular with our feathered friends. Other family members with desirable autumn fruits include the hawthorns (*Crataegus*), crab apples (*Malus*), those excellent wall shrubs *Cotoneaster* and *Pyracantha*, and, of course, roses themselves (the fruits of *R. rugosa* are portly, pot bellied receptacles, while those of *R. moyesii* resemble ancient terracotta vessels). These also have first-rate berries: hollies (*Ilex*); some *Viburnum*, including the wayfaring tree (*V. lantana*) and guelder rose (*V. opulus*); and a few spindles (*Euonymus*), including 'Red Cascade' (a cultivar of *E. europaeus*). Among the dogwoods (*Cornus*), the Asian *C. kousa* and *C. capitata* bear big, pinky-red fruits (the colour of an overripe strawberry) – well liked by blackbirds.

FLAMING FOLIAGE
Yellow and peachy toned leaves

Birch (*Betula*); katsura (*Cercidiphyllum japonicum*, which has the bonus of smelling like burnt sugar); maidenhair tree (*Ginkgo biloba*); larch (*Larix*); swamp cypress (*Taxodium distichum*); dawn redwood (*Metasequoia glyptostroboides*); tulip tree (*Liriodendron tulipifera*). Some of the Japanese maples (cultivars of *Acer japonicum* and *A. palmatum*) also take on custardy tones. These are the best for a smaller garden, and need a sheltered position and protection from late spring frosts, which may harm their fragile new leaves.

The guelder rose (*Viburnum opulus*) produces shiny, intensely red berries. Birds love them.

Excess sugars in the leaves of this Japanese maple produce the brilliant anthocyanins which dye the leaves red in autumn.

Red, orange and maroon leaves
- Trees and shrubs: Japanese maples – 'Osakazuki' is reputed to be the reddest; smoke bush (*Cotinus*); spindle (including *Euonymus europaeus* 'Red Cascade'); witch alder (*Fothergilla major*); witch hazel (*Hamamelis*); sweet gum (*Liquidambar styraciflua*); Persian ironwood (*Parrotia persica*); some cherries (*Prunus*); stag's horn sumach (*Rhus typhina*); rowans and whitebeams (*Sorbus*); *Viburnum.*
- Climbers: Virginia creeper and Boston ivy (*Parthenocissus quinquefolia* and *P. tricuspidata*); crimson glory vine (*Vitis coignetiae*).

AUTUMN WORK
This is the season when the garden is overcome by senescence (a softly sibilant word that nicely mimics the sound of leaves falling). In other words, there is suddenly a lot of dead plant material. Don't be in a hurry to do a thorough clean-up job. Fallen leaves and dried stems offer homes for invertebrates, which will feed the birds, while seed heads are full of nutritious morsels of food – both animal and vegetable.

Do clear leaves off lawns, though, as they obstruct light and air. If the grass is still growing, you can mow with the leaves *in situ* and use the resulting mowings as a mulch for vegetable beds (or any beds that you wish to protect over winter: rain on bare soil can cause surface panning).

If you have an excess of leaves, make leafmould.

Remove fallen leaves from the garden pond also. Some people throw a leaf-catching net over the surface, but this can prevent birds from bathing and drinking, and can also act as an unintentional trap.

Late-flowering meadows should be cut when the flowers have run to seed, in September or early October. Let the cuttings lie for a couple of days to allow the seeds to fall off. Then remove elsewhere, so that the ground does not become over-rich. New meadows and lawns may also be sown now – although not on heavy, clay soil.

Collect seed from ornamental and edible plants that you want to grow

Members of the umbellifer family (*Apiaceae*) often have good skeletons. When cleaning up in autumn, leave them intact so that they may enhance the winter picture and provide food for birds.

more of next year (remember that the seed of F1 hybrid strains is not suitable for saving).

Apples and pears can be harvested: the latter should be picked when still a little unripe. Choose only unblemished fruits for storage in a cool place. If you have plenty of space, they can be stored in boxes in a single layer, so that the fruits are not touching. Otherwise, wrap singly in newspaper, and check regularly to make sure that there is no seepage through the paper from rotting fruits.

Hardy annuals may be sown in the first half of autumn, directly into the ground, or into pots or modules. Sweet peas should be sown in pots. Perennials may be planted now, or lifted and divided, while there is still some warmth in the soil. They will make little top growth, but the roots will be establishing underground.

Sow spring cabbage, hardy salad leaves, oriental greens, Swiss chard and spinach in the first part of autumn.

Plant spring bulbs in autumn (and into winter, if you run out of time). Plant bare-root shrubs and trees in the latter half of the season, and into winter. Plant hedges and soft fruit, if you are not in a cold and damp area – otherwise, wait until spring.

RESOURCES

'If you have a garden and a library, you have everything you need.'
Marcus Tullius Cicero

Further reading

The following are books to which I refer constantly, or which have been a great help to me as a gardener.

Val Bourne, *The Natural Gardener*, Frances Lincoln, 2004

Helen Dillon, *Helen Dillon's Garden Book*, Frances Lincoln, 2007

Charles Dowding, *Organic Gardening: The Natural No-Dig Way*, Green Books, 2007

Charles Dowding, *Salad Leaves for All Seasons*, Green Books, 2008

Andrew Halstead and Pippa Greenwood, *Royal Horticultural Society Pests & Diseases*, Dorling Kindersley, 1997

The Hillier Manual of Trees & Shrubs, David & Charles, 1995

Klaus Laitenberger, *Vegetables for the Irish Garden*, Milkwood Publishing, 2010

Joy Larkcom, *Creative Vegetable Gardening*, Mitchell Beazley, 2008

Joy Larkcom, *Grow Your Own Vegetables*, Frances Lincoln, 2002

Tony Lord (consultant editor), *RHS Plant Finder*, Dorling Kindersley, 2010 (published annually)

Oran O'Sullivan and Jim Wilson, *Ireland's Garden Birds: How to Identify, Attract & Garden for Birds*, The Collins Press, 2008

Graham Rice (editor-in-chief), *Royal Horticultural Society Encyclopedia of Perennials*, Dorling Kindersley, 2006

Matthew Wilson, *Royal Horticultural Society New Gardening: How to Garden in a Changing Climate*, Mitchell Beazley, 2007

Gardening websites

Garden Organic, the British organic growing organization: *www.gardenorganic.org.uk*

Royal Horticultural Society, Britain's largest gardening organization: *www.rhs.org.uk*

The Irish Garden magazine, expert advice, blogs and an online community of gardeners: *www.garden.ie*

Grow It Yourself Ireland, local food growing network, with advice, articles and community forums: *www.giyireland.com*

Charles Dowding's no-dig, organic veg-growing website: *www.charlesdowding.co.uk*

Wildlife websites
The Bat Conservation Trust: *www.bats.org.uk*
The Royal Society for the Protection of Birds: *www.rspb.org.uk*
BirdWatch Ireland: *www.birdwatchireland.ie*
British Trust for Ornithology: *www.bto.org*
Buglife: The Invertebrate Conservation Trust: *www.buglife.org.uk*
Bumblebee Conservation Trust: *www.bumblebeeconservation.org.uk*
The Bumblebee Pages: *www.bumblebee.org*
Butterfly Conservation (UK): *www.butterfly-conservation.org*
Butterfly Ireland: *www.butterflyireland.com*
Irish Butterflies: *www.irishbutterflies.com*
Froglife: *www.froglife.org*
Wild About Gardens (a Royal Horticultural Society and Wildlife Trusts partnership):
  www.wildaboutgardens.org.uk

Sustainability websites
Mother Earth News: 'The Original Guide to Living Wisely', an American magazine devoted
  to self-sufficiency and sustainability: *www.motherearthnews.com*
Ethical Trading Initiative, an organization promoting fair conditions for easily exploited
  workers across the world: *www.ethicaltrade.org*
Freecycle, a worldwide network with thousands of local groups devoted to keeping good
  things out of landfill: *www.freecycle.org*
Friends of the Earth, the world's largest grassroots environmental network:
  www.foei.org (international website with links to national groups)

Specialist seed companies and organizations
Brown Envelope Seeds, Ardagh, Church Cross, Skibbereen, Co. Cork;
  www.brownenvelopeseeds.com
Irish Seed Savers Association, Capparoe, Scarriff, Co. Clare; *www.irishseedsavers.ie*
The Organic Centre, Rossinver, Co. Leitrim; *www.theorganiccentre.ie*
Thomas Etty, Seedsman's Cottage, Puddlebridge, Horton, Ilminster, Somerset, TA19 9RL;
  www.thomasetty.co.uk
Heritage Seed Library, c/o Garden Organic, Coventry, Warwickshire, CV8 3LG;
  www.gardenorganic.org.uk
The Organic Gardening Catalogue, Riverdene Business Park, Molesey Road, Hersham,
  Surrey, KT12 4RG; *www.organiccatalog.com*
The Real Seed Catalogue, Real Seeds, PO Box 18, Newport near Fishguard, Pembrokeshire
  SA65 0AA; *www.realseeds.co.uk*

INDEX

Page numbers in italics refer to illustrations.

ACKNOWLEDGEMENTS

Generous friends, fellow gardeners and many other people helped me with this book.

I am profoundly grateful to Mary Davies for reading every single word before publication, and for commenting with tact and wisdom. She also schooled me in the mysterious craft of indexing. I owe barrow-loads of thank yous to Frances MacDonald, who read several sections and offered many suggestions – and who coaxed, inspired, and organized me with warmth and humour.

I cannot thank Grainne Devaney enough for being such a thoughtful and precious friend to my garden and to me.

I am indebted to Pam Joyce, who brings kindness and order to our house; and to my friend Paul Cox, for his calmness in the face of falling trees and swarming bees.

Joy Larkcom has been a good friend and mentor, as has her husband, Don Pollard. Helen Dillon has given me endless advice, encouragement and entertainment, while robin-charmer Val Dillon has been unfailingly hospitable.

I am grateful to fellow writer Eric Harlacher for his superb counsel, and for cheering me on and up; to Rebekah Burke for baking; and to Romy Burke for being.

I am thankful to Fidelma Farley and Mary O'Callaghan at Oscailt, to Emma Philbin Bowman, who pointed the way there, and to Kirsten Doherty for joining me there and on the Dart.

Frank Franklin, our postman of many years, died before his time, and I regret that I cannot thank him personally for being staunch, dependable and thoughtful. He is missed every day.

Thanks also to my friends and neighbours who have encouraged me from near and far: Koraley Northen, Bob Groves, Mary Dowey, John Grenham, Sara Macken, Judith Spring, Paula Murphy, Máirín Coleman, Trudy Hunt, Ena Prosser, Frank Miller, Paddy Woodworth, Valerie Coyne, Rob Dalton, Jonny Taylor, Jane Ebrill, Ann Sloan, Chris Cotton. Thanks also to Milo de Paor and Lily Hession. And big thanks too to the members of my book club, for being such good sports, for collecting corks for a mulching project, and for putting up with my spasmodic appearances while I have been working on my own books.

Mount Usher Gardens, Co. Wicklow.

For providing information on various subjects, I am grateful to Niall Hatch from BirdWatch Ireland, Dr Eugenie Regan from the National Biodiversity Data Centre, Leona Janson-Smith at the Mayor of London's Press Office, Klaus Laitenberger, Annie Gatti, Iain MacDonald, Graham Rice, Charles Dowding, Hugh Blaisdell, Tom Blaisdell, Dave Devaney, Paul Gaster, Assumpta Broomfield and Kate Bradbury. I am also indebted to the eccentric and irreverent gardening community on Twitter for friendship, and for specialist knowledge on everything from worms to wine.

At the *Irish Times*, I am lucky to work with a great collection of friendly, funny and kind people. I am especially grateful to my editor, Patsey Murphy, for asking me to write about gardens and gardening at a time when it was the one thing I wanted to do more than anything else in the world; to Carmel Daly, who has helped me in so many ways; and to Marie-Claire Digby, Laurence Mackin, Conor Goodman and Orna Mulcahy for forbearance and support over the years.

John Fitzpatrick and Siobhan Mullett introduced me to John Nicoll and Jo Christian at Frances Lincoln, my dream publisher. I am flattered that they asked me to write this book, and that they didn't mind that I wanted to take the photos too. Jo has been especially enthusiastic, wickedly funny and supportive, while Becky Clarke and Nicki Davis have made my words and pictures into a beautiful book. Anne Askwith did a graceful, precise and thoughtful job of copy-editing.

I owe a big thank you to all the people who allowed me to photograph their gardens, and then drink their tea and eat their food: Frances and Iain MacDonald, the Bay Garden, Camolin, Co. Wexford; the Perry family, Glebe Gardens, Baltimore, Co. Cork; the Jay and Pratt families, Anthony McCann and Sean Heffernan, Mount Usher Gardens, Ashford, Co. Wicklow; the Walker family, Fernhill Gardens, Sandyford, Co. Dublin; June Blake, Tinode, Blessington, Co. Wicklow; Paul Newman, Ballintaggart Stud, Colbinstown, Co. Kildare; Jimi Blake, Hunting Brook, Blessington, Co. Wicklow; Elizabeth Temple, Salthill Gardens, Mountcharles, Co. Donegal; TJ Maher, Patthana, Kiltegan, Co. Wicklow; Philip Hollwey, Blackrock, Co. Dublin; Helen and Val Dillon, Ranelagh, Dublin; the Office of Public Works and Seamus O'Brien, Kilmacurragh Botanic Gardens, Kilbride, Co. Wicklow; Tanguy and Isabelle de Toulgoët, Dunmore Country School, Durrow, Co. Laois; Joy Larkcom and Don Pollard, Lislevane, Bandon, Co. Cork.

I owe much to my late mother, Betty Wahl Powers, for showing me that there is abundant happiness in a well mulched vegetable garden, and to my late father J.F. Powers, and my late sister, Mary Farl Powers – a pair of perfectionists – for making me try harder. My sister Katherine A. Powers has been a formidable force, delivering many transatlantic orders and encouragements.

And finally, I am forever indebted to my husband, Jonathan Hession, who has been a non-stop and many-skilled ally: cooking, driving, shopping, log-splitting, chicken-wrangling, dog-walking, photography-teaching, and sorting out so many last sentences (but not the next one). Without him, I would not have been able to make this book.